CESAR CHAVEZ HIGH SCHOOL
8501 HOWARD DRIVE
HOUSTON, TX 77017

Straight Talk About Date Rape

Susan Mufson, C.S.W., and Rachel Kranz

Houston I.S.D.

■® Facts On File, Inc. High School Library
8501 Howard Drive
Houston, TX 77017

Straight Talk About Date Rape

Facts On File, Inc.
11 Penn Plaza
New York, NY 10001

Library of Congress Cataloging-in-Publication Data
Mufson, Susan.
    Straight talk about date rape / Susan Mufson and Rachel Kranz.
        p. cm.
    Includes index.
    Summary: Discusses the phenomenon known as acquaintance, or date, rape, describing situations in which it occurs, how to avoid this crime, and where to get help if you have been a victim.
    ISBN 0-8160-3752-3 (pbk) (alk. paper)
    1. Acquaintance rape—United States—Juvenile literature.
    2. Rape—United States—Prevention—Juvenile literature.
    [1. Acquaintance rape. 2. Rape. 3. Dating violence.] I. Kranz, Rachel. II. Title.
    HV6561.M84 1993
    362.88′3—dc20   92-41681

Facts On File books are available at special discounts when purchased in bulk quantities for businesses, associations, institutions or sales promotions. Please call our Special Sales Department in New York at 212/967-8800 or 800/322-8755.

You can find Facts On File on the World Wide Web at
http://www.factsonfile.com

Cover design by Smart Graphics

Printed in the United States of America

MP FOF 10 9 8 7 6 5 4 3 2 1

This book is printed on acid-free paper.

Contents

1

Date and Acquaintance Rape: Growing Problems

Is It a Crime?

Consider the following situations. Which of them seem like crimes? Which seem like normal, acceptable behavior?

Terry is walking down the street, wearing jeans and a loose cotton shirt. It's about nine o'clock at night, and she's on her way home from the library. Suddenly, a man she has never seen before jumps out of the bushes and grabs her by the arms. She screams and struggles, but no one hears her. He hits her to make her stop screaming. Then he drags her into the bushes, threatens her with a knife, pins her to the ground, and forces her to have sex with him. Afterward, he lets her go home.

Lydia is home alone, studying. Her parents have gone to the movies and her little brother is at a friend's house. It's a hot night, so she's wearing only a light T-shirt. There's a knock on the door, and she answers it. It's Mr. Gonzales, a friend of her father's. Lydia has known Mr. Gonzales since she was a little girl, and he has been a guest in their house many times. When he asks if he can come in and wait for her parents, she lets him in. Then she goes to her room to get a bathrobe. Mr. Gonzales follows her, even though she hasn't asked him to. When she asks him to leave her room, he won't. He shuts the door behind him and pins her down on the bed. Lydia says, "No. don't," but Mr. Gonzales doesn't get up. Instead, he forces her to have sex with him. Then he leaves the apartment, warning Lydia that if she tells her parents, he'll tell them that *she* seduced *him.*

Paul and Jennifer have been going out for about a year. Paul asks Jennifer out on a special date. He's been looking forward to it for weeks. When he comes to pick her up, he sees she's dressed in a low-cut blouse and a short, tight skirt. He takes her out to dinner at the town's best restaurant, then on to front-row seats at a rock concert (it took him weeks to save up the money). Paul pays for everything—Jennifer doesn't even offer, and he wouldn't accept if she did. After the concert, he drives her out to the lake, a good 15 miles out of town. He takes out a six-pack from the back seat of the car and they each have a few beers. They make out for a while, and Jennifer keeps saying how good it feels. In fact, she's the one who puts Paul's hands on her breasts. Then Paul tries to go further. Jennifer says, "No, don't," and tries to push him away, but Paul is stronger than she is and pins her down to the seat of the car. They have sex. Then he takes her home.*

Did you think any of these situations was a crime? Did you think all of them were? In fact, all of these situations are

---

* Although all of the incidents described in this book are based on real situations, the only ones that actually happened are those identified with first and last names or with the name of a town or a college. The other characters are *composites*—fictional portraits that combine elements from many real-life events.

considered rape. The only difference was that Terry experienced *stranger rape,* Lydia experienced *acquaintance rape,* and Jennifer experienced *date rape.*

Of course, the three situations were different as far as the kind of relationship each woman had with the man before the crime occurred. Terry had never met her attacker, and Jennifer had been involved in an intimate romantic relationship with the man who raped her. However, the three cases were the same in one very important respect. In all three, a woman was forced by a man to have sex against her will. That makes it rape, which is a crime.

All rape is serious. In this book, however, we are going to focus especially on date rape and acquaintance rape. *Date rape* is the rape that occurs when a woman has agreed to go out on a date with a man. *Acquaintance rape* includes date rape, but it also includes all rapes that take place between two people who know each other. We'll also talk about *sexual aggression*—ways of forcing a person to have sex that don't fit the definition of rape but are nevertheless extremely serious and damaging.

Both boys and girls can be victims of rape or sexual aggression. Boys or men can rape other boys or men; both girls and boys can exercise sexual aggression against boys. Because the overwhelming majority of all cases of rape and sexual aggression are exercised by boys or men against girls or women, most of the time we'll use the female pronouns *she* and *her* to denote the target. However, we'd like you to remember that much of what we're talking about can apply to boys as well—and in every chapter we'll have a special section for male victims of rape or sexual aggression.

Is Date Rape a New Crime?

Date rape is not exactly a new crime. For about a hundred years now, men and women have been "dating" in the modern sense—going out to spend time with each other without chaperones or parents, often with some kind of sexual involvement, from kissing to intercourse. (Before the 1900s, the social contact between unmarried men and women was much more highly regulated, particularly for teenagers, with a lot more supervision from parents or other adults.) And, sad to say, since men and women have been dating, men have been forcing women to have sex while on dates, against the woman's consent.

Although it was never considered acceptable for a man to force a woman into sexual behavior against her consent, such activity wasn't always called "rape." The woman might even have been blamed for not being able to prevent the man's actions. Now we understand that if a man forces a woman to have sex against her will, that counts as rape *even if he already knows her, even if she has agreed to go out with him on a date, even if she has voluntarily had sex with him on other occasions.* We understand that if the forced sex takes place on a date, then it's called "date rape," and it's a crime—just as much of a crime as if the man had been a perfect stranger.

New Perspectives

As our society's understanding of date rape has grown, we have come to see many situations with new eyes. For example, many people had long taken for granted that athletes and rock musicians did not commit rape. After all, so many young women—and young men—were interested in getting to know them! In the past, many people tended to assume that any young person would welcome the chance to have sex with a musical or athletic star, that sex under such circumstances could not possibly be considered rape.

Recently, however, public awareness has shifted, so that we now realize that even a "hero" might be capable of the crime of rape. Just because a young person wants to go to a party or out on a date with a rock star or athlete doesn't mean that she—or he—also wants to have sex. Simply going out on a date or to a party shouldn't make a person "fair game" for doing something she doesn't want to do. If an athlete or rock star uses force to have sex with a young person, it's rape just as much as if he had jumped out of the bushes and used a knife or gun. Likewise, if a person is coerced into having sex when he or she is too drunk or stoned to make a clear decision, that is also rape, because it is taking away a person's ability to make his or her own decision.

This particular awareness may have been sparked by the 1991 rape conviction of boxing star Mike Tyson, who was found guilty of assaulting a young woman with whom he had been out on a date. A jury decided that even though the young woman had gone back with Tyson to his hotel room, she had not consented to sex. Tyson may have been a beloved sports hero—but he did not have the right to force someone into doing something she did not want to do.

With this new awareness comes the realization that date rape may actually be fairly common on the sports circuit, among rock musicians, and in Hollywood circles. Although, of course, there are probably lots of people who would be willing and even eager to have sex with sports, rock, and movie stars, that does not give those stars the right to force themselves on people who do not consent to sex.

The very idea that a woman might choose to say yes to a date, yes to kissing, even yes to making out, but no to intercourse or other sexual acts is a fairly new idea. Traditionally, women have been viewed as either "good women," who say no to all sexual contact, or "bad women," who have given up their right to say no. The idea that women might enjoy sexual contact but also want to make their own decisions about it is one idea that has helped us become aware of the problem of date rape.

It's also a new idea that a man might not want sex "all the time" or "with anyone he can get" so that he, too, might be forced into sexual situations against his will. A woman who pressures a man to have sexual contact that he doesn't want or is not ready for may also be guilty of sexual aggression, rather than the traditional view that she is "doing the guy a favor" or that he is "crazy not to take advantage of the offer."

These new ideas have given rise to the understanding that date rape and other kinds of sexual aggression do exist, that rape may occur between people who know each other, even like each other, as well as between strangers. As we have become aware that date rape *is* a problem, we have also started to realize just how widespread a problem it really is.

Is Acquaintance Rape a New Crime?

Just as date rape has existed for as long as men and women have been dating, so has acquaintance rape existed for much of the time that men and women have known each other. As with date rape, what is new is not the act itself, but the recognition that the act is a crime.

For years, the myths that existed about rape prevented many people from recognizing it in all the places where it occurred. Some people, for example, maintained that a woman could not be forced into sex against her will unless a weapon was involved. Since an acquaintance was less likely than a stranger to approach a rape victim with a traditional weapon, this led many people to assume that the forced sex that occurred was not really rape.

Other people believed that if a woman had anything to do with the circumstances in which she was raped—for example, if she invited a family friend into her home or offered a delivery man a glass of water on a hot day—then the act didn't count as "rape." In fact, since a woman would be far less likely to expect rape from an acquaintance she would be far more vulnerable to acquaintance rape than to stranger rape—but until recently, society did not recognize the acquaintance rape as a crime.

In her 1929 novel *Ex-wife*, author Ursula Parrott describes an early instance of acquaintance rape: her 1920s divorced heroine meets a man at a party and accepts a date to go dancing with him but makes it clear that she never wants to have sex with him. She realizes that there is something suspicious about the man and decides not to see him again. Later, another man, who seems quiet and shy, invites the woman back to his apartment, where the two of them have a quiet drink. Then the first man shows up and the heroine realizes that the apartment actually belongs to him. The first man, strong and determined, forces the heroine to have sex with him. She realizes that if she fights or tries to run away, she might get beaten up, so she submits. She realizes, too, that if she goes to the police, they will not take her complaint seriously: she has been drinking, she is divorced (i.e, not a virgin), and she is known to date several men.

Although the term acquaintance rape did not exist in 1929, Ursula Parrott described a striking example of the phenomenon in her novel. We can see that what is new is not the fact of acquaintance rape, but the name. Although Parrott portrayed her heroine's pain and anger at what happened to her, she didn't call it "rape."

How Common Are Date and Acquaintance Rape

Have you ever had the experience of learning a new word or finding out the name of a new movie star—and then all of a sudden you are hearing that word or that person's name everywhere? Date and acquaintance rape are a little like that. Once society identified that these types of rape exist and that they are a problem, we began to realize that they occur to far more people than we ever suspected.

For example, a 1989 survey at the University of Massachusetts, Amherst, found that some 13 percent of undergraduates had been the victims of date rape, while another 10 percent were victims of attempted rape. A full 7 percent of these women in the survey said that men had used physical force against them. (The rest of the women had presumably been raped by threat of physical force or by being overcome with drugs or alcohol so that they could not make a clear distinction.)

The study, conducted by sociologist Michael Shively, found that some 26 percent of the women surveyed experienced "sexual coercion"—some kind of strong pressure to engage in sexual behavior that they didn't really want. And 64 percent of the women Shively surveyed were victims of "sexually offensive behavior"—unwanted sexual advances that fell short of actual intercourse.

These findings were supported by Mary Koss, professor of family and community medicine at the University of Arizona and author of *I Never Called It Rape: The Ms. [magazine] Report on Recognizing, Fighting, and Surviving Date and Acquaintance Rape.* In her survey of 32 campuses, she found that 25 percent of the female college students she surveyed were victims of rape or attempted rape. And one out of twelve college men—8 percent—admitted to committing rape or attempted rape.

Koss believes that her own figures probably underestimate the problem. She points out that less than 5 percent of all rape victims report the crime to the police (and many researchers believe that figure is even lower when the rapist is an acquaintance or a date rather than a stranger). Sometimes that's because the women just want to forget about the incident. Other times, they fear they won't be treated well by the police. Still other times, they may not consider what happened to be "rape," especially if they knew or were dating the man involved. Therefore, Koss believes, many women in her survey may not have wanted to admit that they were raped; many other women may not even have realized that they were raped.

"Rape by a stranger tends to be more forceful," Koss comments, "but the psychological effects [of date or acquaintance rape] are just as devastating. One out of every three women who are date-raped consider suicide."

In 1990, Cornell University professor Andrea Parrot released similar findings. She announced that 5 percent of men on college campuses force their dates to have sex, and that up to 25 percent of the women on a college campus will experience rape or attempted rape. Parrot, the author of *Coping With Date Rape & Acquaintance Rape*, says that part of the problem is that the men involved don't consider their actions to be rape. "They think the women don't mean no," Parrot explains. "The men rape and think they did her a favor. All she needed was a push."

Parrot says that not realizing how common date rape is may actually be dangerous: "Women who don't think they are at risk, precisely are at risk because they don't look for signs. They think it happens to someone else."

Still more evidence comes from the pamphlet *"Friends" Raping Friends*, a guide financed by the Ford Foundation and circulated by the Association of American Colleges. According to this guide, one in eight—or 12 percent—of all college women was raped by someone she knew. The problem occurs on virtually every campus in America.

At Wesleyan University alone, a small college in Middletown, Connecticut, some 20 to 40 rapes were taking place each year according to a 1986 statement of Marea Downes, executive director of the Sexual Assault Crisis Service of Middlesex County. Downes believed that at least three-quarters of the Wesleyan rapes were date rapes.

In the November 16, 1986 *New York Times* story that quoted Downes, a female college freshman at Wesleyan was also quoted as saying that she had been raped by her high school boyfriend. She went on to describe the psychological consequences: "After the rape I felt that control had been taken away from me. I couldn't get out of the relationship. I had trouble making decisions. I thought that if I said no it wouldn't mean anything; my body wasn't mine any more."

How many more high school girls experience this problem? Unfortunately, statistics on that age group aren't readily available, but experts in the field believe that the problem of date rape extends to high school girls as well. After all, as Andrea Parrot points out, approximately one in four women will experience rape or attempted rape at some point in her lifetime. Some 82,000 rapes are reported in the United States each year—and, according to the FBI, only about one in ten rapes is ever reported. Parrot believes that when the rapist is not a stranger, that figure goes down to one in a hundred.

One study did ask college students about their experiences in both college and high school. In 1987, psychologist Charlene L. Muehlenhard and undergraduate Melaney A. Linton asked more than 600 college men and women about both their most recent dates and their worst experiences with sexual aggression against women. They defined "sexual aggression" more broadly than rape, as any time a woman was forced to participate in any sexual act, from kissing to intercourse, against her will. More than three-quarters of the women and more than half of the men admitted that sexual aggression against women had occurred on at least one of their dating experiences, either in high school or in college. Nearly 15 percent of the women and 7 percent of the men said that the aggression had taken the form of intercourse against the woman's will.

Carol Sousa, cofounder of the Dating Violence Intervention Project, believes that as many as one in ten teenage girls faces some form of violence in her dating situation, from name-calling and verbal abuse, to hitting and physical threats, to being beaten up or raped. Sometimes, says Sousa, a boyfriend gets a sense of power from making increasingly bigger demands on his girlfriend, forcing her to perform sexual acts against her will just to experience his own power. The girl may think of the boy's demands as an expression of love, but she is also feeling her own sense of powerlessness as she is unable to act according to her own wishes and principles.

Writer Naomi Wolf has a chilling phrase to describe the prevalence of date rape: She says it's "more common than left-handedness, alcoholism, and heart attacks." If Wolf, the author of *The Beauty Myth: How Images of Beauty Are Used Against Women*, is correct, that means that chances are as likely that you know someone who has experienced date rape as that you know someone who is left-handed.

I Never Called It Rape

Is it possible to be raped and not know it? Robin Warshaw thinks it is. Warshaw is the author of a book entitled *I Never Called It Rape.* She found that many women who had been raped by men they knew simply didn't call the event "rape," even though they had in fact been forced to have sex against their will. Warshaw found that the older women she interviewed were more likely to call their experiences "rape." Younger women tended to be more confused, unwilling to accept that a man they had liked and chosen to date had actually forced them into such a painful situation.

In 1985, Mary Koss surveyed 6,159 college students in a study sponsored by *Ms.* magazine and funded by the National Institutes of Health. She found that 73 percent of the women whose experiences fit the legal definition of rape did not perceive themselves as rape victims.

Perhaps the fact that 27 percent of the women surveyed *did* recognize their situations represents an advance, however. Professor James D. Orcutt and Rebecca Faison of Florida State University studied the National Crime Survey figures of 1973–1985. These survey figures measure the difference between crimes that victims experience and the crimes that they actually report to the police. As we have seen, rape tends to be an especially underreported crime, both because of the way that rape victims are treated in our society and because of the various ways that women—and men—understand, or misunderstand, rape.

According to Orcutt and Faison's 1988 study, the percentage of rapes by non-strangers reported by women to the police doubled in the years covered by the study, from 29 percent in 1973 to 59 percent in 1985. As Orcutt put it, "Women are now more likely to realize that they have been the victims and to take appropriate action by reporting the incident to the authorities."

Orcutt and Faison found that, during the same period, the percentage of women reporting rapes by strangers to the police went from 48 percent to 63 percent. While it seems that women became more willing to take action about rape in general during that period, perhaps a specific increase in awareness of date and acquaintance rape helped raise the reporting of rape by acquaintances.

Perhaps, too, women were both more aware of acquaintance rape and more upset about it because their perceptions of sex roles had changed. Many researchers believe that traditional female and male sex roles help contribute to the prevalence of rape, as well as to our society's tendency to misunderstand when rape has occurred. If we see women as destined to "serve men" or to take orders from them, while we encourage men to be the "king" in their houses or the "boss" of their women, we are less likely to be upset at the idea that a man forced a woman to have sex with him, particularly a woman he was dating or involved with.

Orcutt and Faison found, in fact, that in 1973, traditional sex roles were seen as appropriate by 26 percent of the female first-year students and by 47 percent of the first-year males. By 1985, when reporting of acquaintance rape had almost doubled, only 15 percent of the women accepted traditional sex roles, along with only 30 percent of the men. Perhaps seeing men's and women's roles in new ways helped women respond differently to being raped by the men they knew.

Nevertheless, according to John Briere, assistant professor of psychiatry at the University of Southern California (USC) School of Medicine and a specialist in interpersonal violence, "I think if anything, the information we have on date rape and marital rape [rape of wives by their husbands] is vastly underreported . . ."

2

Where Date and Acquaintance Rape Come From

Why Don't We Recognize Date and Acquaintance Rape?

In our society men and women often deal with each other in ways that help create a climate in which acquaintance rape can occur. The same factors that promote these rapes can also keep people from recognizing that the rapes actually occurred.

Dating Customs

Date rape may sometimes be seen as just a "normal" part of dating, an expected part of the relationship between men and women. One of the reasons we don't always recognize date rape has to do with the spoken and unspoken rules about dating itself. Consider the following dates.

Anthony calls Leslie on the phone and asks her out for Saturday night. He suggests dinner at a restaurant he names, followed by a movie that he has chosen. He comes to her house to pick her up in his car, getting out to open the door for her before getting back into the driver's seat. At the restaurant, Leslie knows that Anthony doesn't have a lot of money, so she waits to see what he orders, in order to figure out how expensive her own order should be. When they get to the movie theatre, there are a couple of other movies playing that Leslie is more interested in seeing than the one Anthony has chosen, but by the time she realizes this, she sees that he has already bought the tickets. As they go in, he takes her arm and steers her to the refreshment counter, where he buys them both a large buttered popcorn. Leslie is on a diet and would rather skip the butter, but she doesn't say anything, although when he offers to buy a drink, she does ask for a diet Coke. After the movie, as they are getting into Anthony's car together, he says, "I thought we'd take a little drive before going home," and they drive to the place where everybody goes to "park." When they get done parking, Anthony drives Leslie home.

Rose calls Martin on the phone and asks him out for Saturday night. She suggests dinner at a restaurant she names, followed by a movie that she has chosen. They meet at the restaurant and have a nice dinner. Afterward, Martin tries to pay for both of them, but Rosa says, "I picked the place, so I'll pay." Martin offers to leave the tip, which Rosa accepts. Then he says he's not really interested in the movie she suggested, so they discuss what they'd both like to see. When they finally agree, Martin pays for the movie tickets, even though Rosa offers to buy her own ticket. When Martin insists on paying for both tickets, Rosa says, "Then I'll get the popcorn." Afterward, Martin says that his parents are out for the evening and asks Rosa to come back to his house with him for a while. He offers to walk her home later. Rosa checks to make sure she has enough money for a cab, just in case she needs one, then goes home with Martin.

Which of the dates you've just read about seems like the way guys and girls go out together most often at your school? Which of them seems like the "best" or the "most fun" date? How would you describe the differences between them?

Here are some differences we notice:

- Who pays
- Who makes the decisions about what to do
- Who has control over the transportation

In the first date we described, Anthony pays for everything—dinner, the movie, even the popcorn. Therefore, Leslie feels uncomfortable about disagreeing with his choices. Courteously, she waits to make sure she isn't spending too much of his money when she orders her dinner in the restaurant. Politely, she keeps back her own preferences when it comes to buying the movie tickets and paying for the popcorn. A whole pattern is set up, in which Anthony makes the choices and Leslie goes along. Anthony might not even realize that Leslie's needs and wishes don't always match his, or he might not think that she has any preferences that are separate from his.

Suppose Leslie did speak up as Anthony was buying the tickets. Imagine that she says something like, "I really don't want to see a horror movie—I'd rather see the latest Eddie Murphy movie."

"Oh, come on, give it a try, I bet you'll like the movie I chose," Anthony might reply. Wanting to make her date happy, Leslie gives in. Afterward, Anthony says, "Now didn't you like that movie I chose?" If Anthony has paid for both tickets, and if Leslie likes him and wants to see him again, she is going to find it very difficult to say no. She is much more likely to say, "It wasn't so bad after I got used to it," or even, "Oh, I had a good time." After all, she doesn't want to hurt his feelings, and she doesn't want to seem ungrateful.

Can you see how this pattern might continue on through the end of the evening? If Anthony wants to have sex and

Leslie doesn't, he has had plenty of practice in getting her to go along with his wishes. He might even think that Leslie has already given him the message that afterward, she won't really be upset—she might even be grateful, just as she has seemed to be about the choice of movie. Under such circumstances, Anthony might feel that forcing sex on Leslie is not that different from persuading her to go to a movie that is not her first choice. By the dating pattern they are both creating, Anthony and Leslie are making it easier for Anthony to commit date rape, and both of them are going to have a harder time recognizing that that's what he did.

Furthermore, since Anthony is doing all of the spending, Leslie seems to be doing all of the "taking." Anthony buys her dinner, a movie ticket, and refreshments at the movie. What does he get in return? Many people, both men and women, might feel that Leslie owes Anthony something in exchange for all the money he has spent on her. Combine that feeling of being owed something with the pattern of Anthony making all the decisions, and you can see how Anthony might think he has a "right" to sex from Leslie. Even if she wants to say no, Leslie might even agree that she does owe Anthony *something*, a feeling that undercuts her ability to say no loudly, clearly, and with no room for misunderstanding. Besides, she's been letting Anthony make all the decisions all evening, hiding her own feelings and preferences out of deference to him. That makes it much harder to stand up at the end of the evening and say, "*This* is one thing I *won't* go along with, no matter what you want."

Even if Leslie had spoken up earlier, and even if Anthony had gone along with her, both of them might feel that he was doing her an even bigger favor than before. Then Anthony would not only be paying for a movie—he'd be buying tickets to something that wasn't even his first choice! Not only would he be buying popcorn, he'd be buying the kind he didn't even like! Under the circumstances, both he and Leslie might feel that Leslie owed him even more. The whole idea that dating is an exchange, in which the man puts out money and the woman puts out sex helps make it easier for men to force sex on women without even realizing that what they're doing is wrong, painful, and unfair.

Compare Anthony and Leslie's date to the evening spent by Martin and Rosa. In that date, both people put out some money, made some of the decisions, and offered some of the compromises. At the end of the evening, neither person could say to the other, "I've gone along with you all night— what about what I want?" or "I've been paying the whole evening, now it's your turn." Both people could be reasonably sure that everything they did was acceptable to two people, not just one. Each person has experienced listening to the other person's feelings as well as speaking up for his or her own wishes. If this is the pattern that has been set, it will be difficult for Martin to force Rosa into something without realizing that that's what he's doing. It will also be more difficult for him to feel that he has the "right" to something that she "owes" him. Rosa, too, will be much more able to say no when she means no, and to feel that she has the right to say no if that's how she feels.

Of course, no matter what patterns of dating, no matter who has paid, no matter who has gotten his or her way during the evening, no one owes sex to anybody else. Even if he has spent his life savings on their special date, Anthony is not entitled to force sex on Leslie if she does not want sex. Even if Leslie has been going along with Anthony all evening, she still has the right to say no and to have her wishes respected. No matter what the woman does or doesn't do *before* saying no to sex, if the man continues to force her *after* she says no, he has the sole responsibility for committing rape.

In other words, no pattern of dating *justifies* date rape. However, some patterns might make date rape more likely. And some patterns might make it harder for one or both people to realize that date rape is in fact what has occurred.

Who's in the Driver's Seat?

Another way the two dates differed was in how transportation was handled. When the man has complete control over transportation, the woman is much more vulnerable. It's no accident that a popular image of being in charge is "being in the driver's seat"!

Traditionally in our society, men have been made responsible for the transportation on a date. If the man has a car, he's supposed to pick the woman up and take her home. If there is no car available, the man is often expected to meet the woman at her home, pay for public transportation or a taxi that they both use, and walk the woman to her door at the end of the evening. Asking a woman to meet him at a designated spot, expecting her to pick *him* up, or leaving her at a public place at the end of the evening would not be considered acceptable dating behavior for a man in many circles.

Ironically, the rules about dating and transportation come from the idea that a woman at night is in danger from stranger rapists and other attackers, men from whom her date is supposed to protect her. And in fact, women are in more danger alone at night than men are. However, in giving over their protection to their dates, they may be risking even greater danger. Sadly, more women are raped by men that they know than are raped by strangers.

If a woman is completely dependent on a man for transportation, she has given over a great deal of power to him. She has literally put him "in the driver's seat" for the evening.

Suppose Anthony didn't even tell Leslie they were going to park until she got in his car with him. She can argue with him—but all the time they are arguing, he is driving her somewhere she doesn't want to go. This gives him real power over her: She can't get our of the car without his permission, unless she takes a big physical risk. It also gives them both more "practice" with the idea that he has the right—or at least the ability—to force her into doing something she doesn't want to do.

Suppose Leslie wants to park with Anthony, but she's ready to leave after an hour, whereas he wants to stay much longer. If Anthony is in charge of Leslie's only means of getting home, she is faced with two unpleasant choices: going along with something she really doesn't want or putting up a much bigger fight than she feels comfortable with. If Leslie knows she can always get home some other way—catch a ride with someone else, take public transportation, call a taxi—she knows that she can back up her wishes with real power over her own movements.

By contrast, on the other date, Rosa made sure she had taxi fare before going to Martin's house. That way, if she didn't like how Martin was behaving, at least she wouldn't have to worry about how she would get home. Both she and Martin were getting the message that Rosa makes her own decisions and has the power to carry them out.

Sugar and Spice Might Not Be Nice

The dating patterns we have been looking at have much deeper roots than simply the history of what men and women do on dates. They spring from our society's traditional ideas about the very identities of men and women, ideas that find expression in the way that girls and boys are brought up.

Naturally, these patterns go beyond dating itself to extend to many situations in which men and women spend time together. Consider the following scenarios.

Ellen is home alone one day when the meter man comes to her family's apartment. She knows the man fairly well, since he always chats with family members when he comes to read the meter on Saturday mornings. Usually Ellen's mother offers him a glass of water or a cup of coffee, and he might even sit down and drink it at the kitchen table before going on to the next apartment.

Because of this custom, Ellen also offers the meter man something to drink when he comes over. She feels a little uncomfortable when he asks her to sit down and have a cup of coffee with him, but she can't really think of any reason why she should feel that way, so she goes along. He moves his chair a little closer to her than she feels comfortable with, and once again she doesn't want to hurt his feelings by saying anything. He makes a few teasing remarks about Ellen and how she looks today and whether she has any boyfriends, and she just smiles, not knowing how to tell him that this kind of talk is making her uncomfortable.

Suddenly, with what seems to Ellen no warning at all, the meter man grabs her and forces her to have oral sex with him. She wants to fight back, but she's worried about getting hurt—and she's worried about how badly she might injure him. After he leaves, she wonders if she was somehow to blame. She didn't think she was giving him a sexual message—being friendly, as she had seen her mother be. She also felt that by offering him coffee and keeping him company while he drank it, she was only being polite and helping a guest to feel comfortable, as she had been taught. Now she worries that other people will see her friendly, polite actions as sexual invitations.

Of course, as we've said before, Ellen is not to blame for the crime that happened—the person who raped her is to blame. However, because she was so concerned with helping the other person feel comfortable, even at her own expense, Ellen had a difficult time protecting herself in what turned out to be a dangerous situation. The types of difficulty she had can be related to the ways that girls are brought up in our society.

The meter man, on the other hand, may not believe that he committed a crime. He may feel that, since he was *able* to force sex on Ellen, he had the *right* to do so. He may see her unwillingness to fight back not as fear of getting hurt but as a secret willingness to have sex. After all, he was willing to get scratched or hit in order to have sex with her! He may have seen the whole encounter as a kind of contest between the two of them, and his attitude to contests might be "Whoever wants to win the most, will win—and deserves to win." This kind of thinking is connected to the way boys tend to be brought up in our society.

Which of the following lists of characteristics would you say is more common to girls? Which would you say is a more accurate description of most boys?

- polite
- puts other people's wishes first
- waits to be invited before giving an opinion
- doesn't like to contradict or disagree
- very nervous about getting physically hurt
- has probably never been in a fistfight
- stays away from tackle sports like football or contact sports like boxing
- feels responsible for making sure "everybody has a good time"

- masterful, a "take-charge" person
- gives opinions and expects others to listen
- has been in at least one fistfight
- may enjoy tackle sports like football or contact sports like boxing
- may not like getting physically hurt but thinks that lots of things are worse (such as backing off from a fight or avoiding a great play in a game)
- feels responsible for deciding what the group should do or for coming up with a plan
- feels responsible for protecting others physically

In general, women are brought up to match more of the characteristics on the first list, while men are brought up to have more of the characteristics on the second list. Of course, there are exceptions to every rule—boys who spend a lot of time worrying about hurting other people's feelings, girls who have no trouble disagreeing with everybody in sight, boys who have never learned to use their fists, girls who have black belts in karate. If you or the people you know don't fit the stereotypes of men and women, boys and girls, congratulations! Most of us, however, recognize at least some traditional reactions in ourselves, even if we have broken out of the stereotypes to some extent.

There are good and bad things about both lists of characteristics. The problem comes when people feel pushed by their training into situations that are bad for them or for other people. For example, girls are often brought up to go along with others, to be afraid of hurting other people's feelings, and to give in to others rather than to get their own way. Sometimes, these are excellent qualities that help groups get along well or make social situations run more smoothly. Sometimes, though, these qualities can lead to a girl's going along with situations that are bad for her. If a guy keeps making decisions that disregard a girl's feelings, she might feel that she has to be nice to him rather than stick up for herself.

Boys, on the other hand, are brought up to have definite opinions, to take charge, offer protection, and put themselves on the line for what they want or believe. These good qualities can help get projects going, promote lively discussions, or encourage people to feel safe. Sometimes, though, a guy might be so concerned with proving himself that he might not leave room for other people's thoughts or feelings, either because he doesn't care about others or because he genuinely doesn't realize that not all people are as good at standing up for themselves as he is.

Furthermore, most boys are encouraged at some point to explore their physical abilities, through sports, through fighting with each other, or both. Most boys have many chances to learn that a little physical pain is not the end of the world, that it's possible to fight physically for what you want. Boys might also have the chance to fight physically with an opponent, to learn that they can hurt someone without killing him or doing permanent damage.

Girls, on the other hand, are strongly discouraged from fistfights or physical expressions of anger or competitiveness almost from their earliest years. They are not generally encouraged to go out for contact sports like boxing or football, and they are often not even pushed toward highly physical team sports like soccer or basketball. Thus many girls don't have the feeling they are capable of using their bodies to fight back. They may not have the sense that even if they get hit or hurt, they will survive and it might be worth it to fight back physically. They may feel that they actually don't have the ability to hurt someone because they don't have the right to hurt someone else. Not having much experience with physical combat, they may worry that if they hit someone, they will seriously hurt the person or even kill him.

Pressure from Inside and Outside

Both boys and girls might feel under a lot of pressure to fit certain sex-role stereotypes. A girl, for example, might think that no guy will like her unless she is "sweet," "good-tempered," "easy going,"and "willing to please." A guy might think that no girl will like him unless he is "forceful," "a-take-charge guy," "tough," and "a winner." Girls might feel that other girls will make fun of them or think they're weird if they don't act as if they're "in love" or don't feel willing to make "any sacrifice" for the guy they're interested in. Guys might feel that other guys will mock them or humiliate them if they don't "score."

All of these patterns contribute to the climate in which date rape takes place. A girl goes out on a date believing that a take-charge guy will pay for her and take care of her. If he turns out to be dangerous or disrespectful, she may feel helpless or at a loss. Meanwhile, a guy goes out on a date believing that he has to be forceful and a winner. He may genuinely believe that a girl will take him more seriously or respect him more if he shows that he is strong enough to get his way. The same type of patterns affect acquaintances as well.

Thinking About Sex

"Nice Girls" and "Real Men"

Besides our general ideas about dating and male/female roles, our society's ideas about sex itself help contribute to the climate in which date and acquaintance rape can take place. One widespread stereotype says that there are two kinds of women: "good girls" who don't like sex and "bad girls" who do.

A "good girl" is supposed to stay a virgin until she's married. She's supposed to say no to a guy's sexual advances, partly in order to keep her virginity, partly because she's not supposed to have any sexual feelings of her own.

On the other hand, a "bad girl" or a "slut" likes sex so much she's not supposed to be able to say no to anybody. Once a girl has a reputation for "doing it," she's supposed to be willing to "do it" with anybody, under any circumstances. And if a girl enthusiastically says yes to some kinds of sexual contact—kissing, making out, petting—rather than saying no all the time, she may also be seen as giving up her right to ever say no.

In our earlier example, for example, when Jennifer put Paul's hands on her breasts, showing that she liked that kind of sexual contact, Paul interpreted her actions to mean that she was a "bad girl" or a "slut" who liked sex, rather than the stereotypical "good girl" who says no all the time. Jennifer wasn't saying yes to intercourse with Paul at that time, she was only saying yes to making out. But because Paul could only see women in two categories—"good girls" and "bad girls"—he couldn't tell the difference between Jennifer's saying yes to making out and her saying no to intercourse.

In this kind of thinking, it's as though girls and women have the right to make only one kind of decision about their sexuality—to say no. Once they say anything else, even once, it's as though they've given up all rights to make any decisions at all. In a way, that's why it's even possible to use the word *girls*—which means female *children*—when we're talking about people who are old enough to have sex. Calling women *girls* is part of a way of thinking that sees women as children rather than as adults with sexual feelings and the right to act on them in whatever way they choose.

Because women are not seen as adults but as girls they are supposed to "need" men to make sexual decisions for them. In many popular movies, books, or television shows, men are shown forcing themselves sexually on women—who afterwards are grateful. In the movie *Gone With the Wind,* for example, heroine Scarlett O'Hara tells the hero, Rhett Butler, that she doesn't want to have sex with him. When Rhett forces her to have sex, she is shown to be literally "swept off her feet" as he carries her into the bedroom. The morning after, she is shown smiling and singing to herself: "She laughed with delight at the sight of his smile, and trembled with fear at his frown." The message this scene gives is precisely the message that encourages date rape: A woman is really a "girl" who needs a "real man" to force her into sexual pleasure. The decision he makes for her is going to be better than the decision she makes for herself.

If women are supposed to stay "girls," boys are taught to see sex as their route to becoming "real men." In this kind of thinking, a guy who doesn't want to have sex with a woman on a particular evening would be called a "baby," a "wimp," or some other word that meant he wasn't a "real man." If "good girls" are supposed to always say no to sex, "real men" are supposed to always want it.

In the same vein, guys talk about sex as "scoring," which also takes the decision making out of sex. A guy is often under a lot of pressure not to think about whether he wants to have a sexual relationship with a woman, or about what kind of sexual contact he wants (just kissing? making out? going all the way?), or about how to make sure that both he and his partner are getting what they want. Instead, a guy is supposed to "go for the gold" every time. After all, you don't have to think about whether or not you want to score when you're playing a game—by definition, you want as many points as possible. So guys may feel under pressure to "push ahead to victory" every time they go out with a woman.

If you combine a guy's pressure to "score" with the belief that a woman really doesn't know what she wants when it comes to sex, or that if she's enthusiastic or sexually active she's a "slut" who has given up the right to say no, you have a bunch of opinions that make date rape seem okay. In that kind of thinking, a woman simply isn't allowed to say no under the following circumstances:

- if she she's not a virgin (as though saying yes to one man means that she must say yes to every man)
- if she's ever had intercourse with that same guy before (as though a person couldn't want to have sex with someone on one night and not want to have sex with the same person on another night)
- if she seems to be enthusiastic about any kind of sexual contact (as though there were no difference between kissing, making out, petting, and intercourse)

Likewise, in that kind of thinking, a guy is never allowed to stop if he has the power to get his way—and "his way" is always supposed to mean intercourse. You can see how these ways of thinking about men, women, and sex help set up the climate in which a guy could force himself on a woman sexually and honestly believe that he wasn't doing anything wrong—even if, in fact, he is committing a crime that will cause the woman a great deal of physical and emotional pain.

Sex Objects and Relationship Objects
Another aspect of the "good girl/bad girl" split is the tendency to see women as "sex objects." In this view, women—or at least "bad girls"—are good for only one thing, to give sexual pleasure to men. Though many or even most men would not necessarily agree with such an arrogant view of

women, and though many women would not agree either, we are all affected by it to some extent.

For example, when a television commercial selling beer or cars shows lots of beautiful women smiling seductively, the only important thing about those women is how desirable they are sexually. And part of what makes them so desirable is the image of how *willing* they seem to be to have sex, either with a man in the commercial or the men watching the commercial at home. The image used to sell the product is the picture of a woman who wants whatever the man wants. She has no desires or wishes of her own—she certainly won't argue with the man about his choice of a movie or say no to intercourse when he wants her to say yes.

Likewise, when women are shown in *Playboy*, in other pornographic magazines, or in pornographic movies, their only important qualities are their sexual attractiveness and their sexual willingness. Someone looking at the picture of a *Playboy* centerfold would probably not be led to think about what kinds of movies she likes, what kind of music she listens to, what she likes to talk about, whom she'll vote for. Even the idea of asking those questions about that type of woman seems silly, doesn't it? Those women's thoughts, feelings, preferences are so unimportant that you can't even connect them with the images that are shown. All that you can imagine is that these are women who would gladly have intercourse—or any other kind of sexual contact that any man might want.

Men who grow up in a society filled with these images—in everyday advertising and movies as well as in pornography—can't help absorbing at least some of the idea that the ideal woman is a "sex object"—a "thing" that exists only to satisfy their sexual needs. Such a climate teaches a man that he has the "right" to expect that type of relationship with a woman he is dating, especially a woman who seems to like him and to want to please him.

Writer Warren Farrell has pointed out that if men are conditioned to see women as "sex objects," women are trained to see men as "relationship objects." In that kind of thinking, a woman doesn't see a man as a whole person, with lots of different feelings, needs, fears, and wishes. Instead, she thinks, this guy would make a good boyfriend because he has lots of money or this guy will make me look good if he's my boyfriend because he's captain of the football team. Guys may judge each other on their ability to "score;" girls often judge each other on their ability to hold high-status boyfriends.

In other words, men and women are trained to see each other in very narrow ways. Men are pressured to think of women as "objects" to meet their sexual needs. Women are encouraged to think of men as "objects" to meet their needs for security, status, or money. Men feel under pressure to "score" and women feel under such pressure to "have great boyfriends" that both sexes find it very difficult to see each other as full human beings.

We believe that this climate is hurtful to both men and women. When this way of thinking results in date rape, however, it is by definition the man who has gotten "his way" while the woman has been forced into an action she did not choose.

Money and Worth

The difference between men and women that we've been talking about are not just "differences." They represent a system of inequality between men and women, a system in which men have some kinds of rights and power that women simply don't have.

One of the most significant ways in which our society measures a person's worth is money. In this climate, the fact that a woman earns only 61 cents for every dollar that a man earns is a telling indication that our society generally values men more than women. Likewise, the fact that men generally hold the higher-status jobs while women hold the lower-status jobs reflects the fact that our society sees men as more powerful and capable than women.

This message is further reinforced by the lack of women in high government positions, such as in the U.S. Senate or holding federal judgeships.

Of course, if you grow up in a society where the majority of the better jobs and leadership positions are held by men, you too might absorb the message that men are somehow "better" than women. At the very least, you might automatically associate power with men and weakness with women.

Test you own assumptions. As you look at the following job pairs, whom do you picture holding each job named—a man or a woman?

doctor—nurse
executive—secretary
college professor—first grade teacher
dentist—dental assistant
director—costume person
accountant—bookkeeper
computer programmer—data-entry person

Generally, the first name in each pair represents the more powerful, prestigious, and higher-paying job—as well as the job more likely to be held by a man. If your images included more variety than this, congratulations! Your thinking has escaped many of our society's more powerful stereotypes. Unfortunately, though, statistics show that in fact, men do predominate in the first job in each pair. Even when we personally know women who have worked some of these jobs, we still might tend to associate those positions with men.

At first glance, the connection between date and acquaintance rape and the lack of women doctors or senators might not seem obvious. Upon further thought, however, we can see that both phenomena are part of a larger problem: a system that values women far less than men, economically, socially, and politically. In such a system, it becomes easier for both men and women to accept that men, rather than women, should "get their way" on a date—even if the man has to commit date rape to do it. Likewise, it becomes easier for men and women to see acquaintance rape as a man's right—as long as he can get away with it.

Symptoms and Diseases

Of course, as we've said before, holding these kinds of attitudes doesn't justify rape. People are responsible for their own actions no matter what reasons or excuses they may have for them. But as we seek to understand why and how rape happens, we need to realize that it comes out of a much bigger system of thinking. It's like the symptom of a much bigger disease. In the end, if rape is to be stopped, we need to understand the disease as well as the symptoms.

When a Man Is the Target

So far, we've been talking about what pressures help support the idea that it's all right for men to force their own sexual preferences onto women. What about when the roles are reversed? What kinds of pressures can help make men the targets of date rape?

When a boy goes out with a girl, both people may buy into the myths we have talked about earlier: that guys should always be ready to "score;" that a guy is supposed to be a protector who "takes care of" a woman, in sexual as well as other ways; that all guys see all women as "sex objects" with whom they should be ready to have sex at any time. If a woman wants to have sex with a man, she may assume that there is no need to find out about his preferences or his timing—he should simply always be ready.

In fact, men are just as different from one another as women are. Every human being has his or her own personal feelings about sex. People are ready for sexual relationships at different ages. Some people see very little emotional difference between making out and having intercourse; other people feel very different about those different steps in sexual intimacy; still other people may feel one way at one age and another way at another age—or their feelings may vary depending on their partner (with Laura, there's no difference between making out, petting, and having sex; with Lillian, the emotional quality of the relationship creates a distinction between these categories).

Men may all be different, each with his own timetable and preferences—but the myths say that "men are all alike." If men feel under pressure from these myths, and if women buy into them, both men and women might believe that a man should "put out" for a woman even if he doesn't want to. A man may worry that if he doesn't have sex, he isn't a "real man." Or he may worry that if he doesn't want to have sex with a particular woman, he might be gay. Because being a gay man (a man who has sexual relationships with other men) is looked down upon and punished in many areas of our society, many men are afraid of being gay. A guy who sees being a "real man" as taking care of a woman might feel obligated to satisfy his date when she wants sex, whether he feels like it or not.

The idea that all men always want sex seems as reasonable as it seemed silly to consider asking what a *Playboy* model thinks about the presidential election—and for the same reasons. These ideas—some women don't have a thought in their head except pleasing men; a man always wants sex and never has to be coaxed or forced into it—are very powerful stereotypes. But in fact, some men— maybe even most men—do *not* fit the stereotypes.

Even if a man doesn't fit the stereotype of the "ever-ready" guy, he may still feel vulnerable to pressure to live up to this image. In fact, he may feel even more pressure than a guy who feels more self-confident. Such a man might pressure himself to give his date what she seems to want, putting himself in sexual situations that he doesn't want or isn't ready for. Or he might be the target of more active pressure from the woman he's dating.

Although women are less likely to threaten men physically or to overpower them with superior force, they can pressure men psychologically. In our definition, this is not rape, but it is sexual aggression, which is also damaging, upsetting, and wrong. A woman might pressure a man by:

- threatening to tell people he's gay;
- threatening to tell people he's a wimp;
- threatening to tell people he's a bad lover;
- making fun of him;
- encouraging him to wonder if there's something wrong with him or his sexuality;
- telling him that he "owes" her something;
- insulting him or finding hurtful things to say to him about his looks, his body, or his sexuality.

There's another way that women might pressure men, which is to play on the idea that women are weak and men are strong. A woman might present herself to a man as so weak and needy that she will suffer greatly or even kill herself if he doesn't give her what she wants. A man who believes he is responsible for protecting or taking care of women might be vulnerable to that type of pressure.

Whether the roles are reversed or not, we believe the targets of sexual aggression should learn how to protect themselves—and that the men or women who are sexually aggressive or who rape should take responsibility for their actions and not force their choices onto others. We think it's important to distinguish between rape (which involves either some form of physical control or physical incapacity, as when the target is too drunk or high to make a rational decision) and sexual aggression (which involves emotional pressure). We also think that both types of attack are extremely damaging, whether a man or a woman is the target.

Of course, if a boy goes out on a date with another boy or man, he may also be subject to sexual pressures, force, or the threat of force. A homosexual boy or man might also rape his date. And an otherwise "straight man" might be guilty of acquaintance rape or stranger rape with a boy or a young man.

Everybody's Problem

Date rape, acquaintance rape, and the social conditions that allow them hurt both men and women, so both men and women should be responsible for taking steps to stop them. In chapters 5 and 6, we'll talk about some of the ways that you can take action to help prevent date and acquaintance rape, both in your own lives and in society as a whole. Here, we'd like to talk about how these rapes hurt us all, and why we all have a stake in stopping them.

Date and acquaintance rape hurt girls in both obvious and not-so-obvious ways. Here are some of the ways we thought of:

Date and acquaintance rape hurt girls by:

- putting them at risk for physical and emotional damage (for more details, see chapter 5);
- encouraging them to mistrust boys;
- teaching them that it's dangerous to express their sexuality or to have sexual needs;
- giving them the overall message that the world isn't a safe place for them and that their rights are restricted.

Can you think of other ways in which date rape hurts girls?

It may not be so obvious how date rape and acquaintance rape hurt boys. But one way that they can hurt boys is by discouraging girls from trusting them. To see how it can hurt boys in other ways, we might need to take a step back and look at the bigger picture. Instead of just talking about date and acquaintance rape, let's talk about the overall climate that produces these rapes—the system that says that men's feelings count and women's don't, that says that a woman's pay should be two-thirds of a man's, that says that "good girls" don't have sex and "real men" want sex all the time. How does that climate of sexual inequality hurt boys?

Sexual inequality hurts boys by:

- demanding that they always do the asking out, always pay on dates, always drive, and always take total responsibility for how the date goes
- presuming that they are "always ready" for sex and ignoring the real and complicated feelings they may actually have
- making them into "relationship objects" that girls judge by their status and wealth, rather than by who they really are
- encouraging a girl to pressure a guy into a long-term monogamous relationship that a guy may not want or be ready for, just so a girl will feel more secure that she has "a man of her own"
- forcing guys to guess what a woman wants sexually, since "good girls" aren't allowed to say what they really want
- encouraging girls to resist them sexually, even when a girl might not want to, for fear of being turned into a "bad girl" who has lost her right to say no.

Can you think of other ways in which sexual inequality hurts boys?

We might add one more subtle way in which boys as well as girls suffer from sexual inequality. In our current system, boys are often given the message that their feelings and wishes are more important than girls'. It's that thinking that helps encourage some boys to commit date and acquaintance rape—the idea that, whether it's a movie or a sexual experience, they "know best" and therefore have the right to force the girl to go along.

At first glance, it might seem that boys *benefit* from that kind of thinking. After all, who wouldn't want his or her way all the time, if that were possible? Why should boys give up the fun of getting their own way, just because girls don't like it?

In fact, that way of thinking can also be a lonely way to see the world. A guy who feels that he has to force a woman to go along with him or who doesn't even notice that he *is* forcing a woman is missing out on the fun of having a woman as a companion and an equal. A guy who has to force sex on a woman is missing out on the fun of having sex with a woman who wants it as much as he does. A guy who is always taking charge is missing out in the fun of letting someone else take care of him for a change.

Sometimes guys feel torn between two different ways of thinking and feeling. One way says that they *should* get whatever they want; another way says that they should take care of other people. A guy who feels torn like that might rape or hit a woman out of frustration or anger—and then later feel terribly guilty at the way he has failed to take care of her and failed to respect her. All of us are only human—if we have license to behave badly, we just might do it, even if we feel bad about it afterward. Creating a system in which men and women are equally respected would take away the men's "license" to rape or attack women—which might be a relief to many men as well as to women.

Finally, the myths and stereotypes that come from sexual inequality put a lot of pressure on guys to be a certain way. Being a "real man" may feel like a strain to many guys, at least some of the time. What if you like doing things that "real men" don't do, such as cooking or sewing? What if you have feelings that "real men" aren't supposed to have, such as getting scared or wanting to cry? What if you feel that girls don't like you enough because you don't measure up to the ideal of the "real man" as well as some of your classmates do? When both men and women are respected as people, both guys and girls get the chance to find out who they really are.

Meanwhile, in our current system of sexual inequality, both men and women live in a world where date and acquaintance rape are extremely common. In the next two chapters, we'll discuss exactly what date and acquaintance rape are and how to identify them. Then we'll go on to talk about ways in which both boys and girls can prevent rape, and how both sexes can deal with the trauma of rape if it does happen. In our final chapter, we'll provide you with hot lines and addresses for organizations that can offer more information, counseling, or concrete help in coping with the problem of date and acquaintance rape.

3

What Is Date Rape?

A lot of the difficulty in dealing with the issue of date rape comes from the confusion about just what it is. Most people can agree that if a woman is walking down the street and a man jumps out at her and sexually attacks her while threatening her with a knife or a gun, that's rape. The arguments start when the man is someone whom the woman knows. And the argument gets even more heated when the woman not only knows the man, but has agreed to go out on a date with him. If a woman has said yes to a date, does that mean she has said yes to sex? If a woman says no, does that really mean yes? Just how is a guy supposed to know what a woman means and what she *really* wants?

Defining Date Rape

Test your own awareness. Which of the following situations do you believe count as date rape? Which are simply poor judgment or bad communication? Why?

Charles and LaToya have been dating for about six weeks, and they seem to like each other a lot. They have done some kissing, but nothing more. One night when they go out, Charles says, "I'm tired of this. If you want to keep seeing me, we'll have to do more." LaToya isn't comfortable with the idea of going further, but she doesn't want to lose Charles, so she agrees to have sex with him. Afterward, she feels creepy and upset, and she knows that for her, what she did was wrong.

Bill asks Lou Ellen out to dinner and a movie. She shows up for the date wearing a miniskirt and a tight, low cut leotard. Bill insists on paying for everything and takes her to a really nice restaurant. During the movie, she leans over and takes Bill's hand, and they hold hands for a while. Afterward, when Bill suggests that they drive out to the lake and sit in his car for a while, Lou Ellen agrees. They kiss for a while, and then Bill starts to pull down her leotard. Lou Ellen says "No, don't." Bill stops for a while, and they kiss for a while longer. Then Bill starts to pull down her leotard again, and again Lou Ellen says no. Bill says, "You can't tease me and get away with it!" Lou Ellen realizes that if she gets out of the car, she has no way to get back home. She's also afraid that if she hits Bill, he'll hit her back. She keeps saying, "No, please, don't," but Bill keeps going until they have had sex.

It's the first time Alicia has gone out with Luis, and he takes her to a party in the basement of a friend's house. People are drinking, and Alicia and Luis each have a couple of beers. Alicia is feeling high and relaxed, and when everyone else starts making out, she and Luis do too. When he starts to go further than she is comfortable with, she says, "Stop! Stop!" But he answers, "You wouldn't be here if you didn't want it." Alicia tries to push him away, but he's stronger than she is. He pins her down to the couch and doesn't let her up until he has finished having sex with her.

Angela and Marco have been dating for about a month. So far, all they've done is kiss a little bit, but Angela isn't satisfied with that. One night when Angela's parents are out, she invites Marco over and takes him to her room. They start to kiss, then Angela gets more aggressive. Marco pulls away, but Angela won't stop. She says, "What's the matter, don't you care about me?" Marco really isn't comfortable going further, but he sees that Angela is hurt and upset, and he feels bad about that. He also feels funny—what kind of guy doesn't want to go all the way? Even though he doesn't think he's ready for it, he goes ahead and has sex with Angela.

In all four of these situations, at least one person is making bad decisions, either by forcing someone into something the other person isn't interested in or by agreeing to something he or she doesn't feel good about. What happens between Charles and LaToya and between Marco and Angela is called *sexual aggression*—putting pressure on someone to have a sexual relationship he or she is not interested in or not ready for. Sexual aggression could include threatening to leave someone if the person doesn't go further with you sexually, crying or getting upset at the other person's limits, or threatening to spread rumors and stories about the person if he or she doesn't go along with your wishes. Sexual aggression can go from pressuring someone into a goodnight kiss through pushing someone to make out or pet to manipulating another person into having sex. Either men or women can be sexually aggressive, although in our culture, it's far more common among men.

Date rape goes one step further than sexual aggression. Date rape occurs when actual physical force or the threat of physical force is used for the man to get his way. In "the threat of physical force" we would include circumstances such as the woman being dependent on the man for a ride home, the woman being isolated and/or outnumbered (such as being alone with the man at his house or being at a party with lots of the man's friends and none of her own), or any other circumstance in which the woman realizes that she cannot back up her "no" with the physical power to take care of herself. (There have been a very few cases of females raping males, but there are such rare exceptions that we'll continue to focus on date rape as something that boys do to girls.) Bill and Lou Ellen, Luis and Alicia, are examples of date rape.

Date rape also occurs when a woman is not capable of making her own decisions because she is drunk, high, or asleep. A man who takes advantage of the fact that a woman is not physically or mentally able to say no to him is committing rape. Likewise, if the girl is too young to know what is happening, is mentally retarded, or is incapable of making a decision for some other reason, having sex with her is considered rape. (In some states, sex with a girl below a certain age is known as *statutory rape*, because a law, or *statute*, says that any kind of sex with this underage girl is rape by definition.)

To put it simply, *date rape takes place whenever a boy uses force or the threat of physical force to coerce a girl with whom he is on a date into having sex, or whenever a boy has sex on a date with a girl who is not capable of saying no.* While "sex" is usually defined legally as the penetration of the penis into the vagina, we would also include anal sex (penis to anus [rear opening]) and oral sex (penis to mouth or mouth to vagina). In other words, when a boy uses physical force or the threat of it to commit one of these acts, he is guilty of rape.

"Special Circumstances"

Do the surrounding circumstances matter when it comes to defining date rape? We don't believe they do. Might doesn't make right. If a girl says no, her wishes should be respected even if she doesn't have the physical strength to back those wishes up.

Jerry Prieto puts the matter even more clearly. Prieto is a sergeant on the police force of the University of California at Long Beach. His job duties include giving all-male work-shops to the students on his campus. He tells the men that once a woman says no—even if it's in the middle of a sex act—then anything that follows is a crime. Even if a woman's no means that she is changing her mind, she still has the right to have that no respected.

A disturbing study by Washington State University psychologist Gloria Fischer shows that many college students are willing to make excuses for men who force sexual intercourse on women. In Fischer's survey, students were given the following scenario:

> A male and female college student go out on a date. Afterwards, they enter his apartment and sit in front of the fireplace, sipping wine. He kisses her and, even though she resists his advances, uses his superior strength to force her into having sex.

When given this scenario in the absence of any other information, some 85 percent of the college students said yes, that was rape. But then, many of them felt that their answer would change depending on one or more of the following nine circumstances:

- if he had spent a lot of money on her
- if she had gotten him sexually excited
- if she had let him touch her breasts
- if they had dated each other for a long time
- if she was drunk or stoned
- if she was going to have intercourse with him and had then changed her mind
- if she had had intercourse with other males
- if she had led him on
- if he was so sexually excited he couldn't stop

Some 13 percent of the students surveyed said that to them, these circumstances didn't make any difference—rape was rape. And in a companion high school survey, 44 percent of the females and 24 percent of the males agreed. They all believed that no matter what the surrounding circumstances were, a woman's no means no, and that women have the right to say no even if they don't have the physical strength that men do.

These survey results were supported by another study, conducted among 106 male students at Texas A&M and Indiana Universities, and reported by Andrea Parrot in her book *Coping With Date Rape & Acquaintance Rape.*

The study gave the men three different descriptions of dates. In some descriptions, the man did the asking; in others, the woman did. In some descriptions, the man paid for the date; in others, the woman paid or both people shared in the expenses. The imaginary couples went to various places on their dates, but in at least one story, they went to the man's apartment.

Then the men were asked to decide whether the circumstances of a date ever justified forced sex. As in the other study we described, many men believed that some circumstances did justify ignoring a woman's wishes. For example, the men believed that forced sex was justified when the man paid, perhaps going on the theory that the woman then "owed" him something in return. They also believed that forced sex was justified when the couple went to the man's apartment, perhaps believing that any woman who agreed to be alone with a man was giving up her "good girl" protection. And many of the men in this study believed that forced sex was justified if the woman had asked the man out.

A third study, also reported by Andrea Parrot, was conducted among teenagers by researchers at the University of California, Los Angeles (UCLA). In this survey, 54 percent of the boys surveyed said that forced sex was acceptable if a woman first said yes to intercourse and then changed her mind. Another large group of boys said that if the woman said yes to kissing, they might assume she was saying yes to intercourse, unless she was very, very specific about what she was saying yes to.

As in the other two studies, the boys in the UCLA study felt that forced sex would be okay if the man had spent a lot of money on the woman—that is, almost 40 percent of them did. Once again, dates were being seen as an exchange in which the man puts out money and the woman puts out sex. Furthermore, over half of the boys in the UCLA study felt that a man had a right to sex if the woman had "led him on." Finally, the UCLA study found that over one-third of the boys interviewed believed that a guy has a right to force sex on a girl if he's so turned on that he "thinks he can't stop."

The problem with allowing these other circumstances to influence thinking about date rape is that they grow out of some very old—and very false—myths about men and women. Although the myths are not true, they have had tremendous power in affecting the way we think about men, women, sex, and rape.

Myths and Facts About Men and Women

Myth: If a girl dresses up in a sexy way, she is as good as telling a guy that she wants to have sex with him.

Fact: If a girl dresses up in what you think is a sexy way, there are lots of messages she might be giving you. She might be saying that she wants you to think she's sexy—to admire her good figure or her physical freedom. But she might just be saying that she wants to be admired and appreciated for her stylish flair. Sometimes the latest looks include short skirts, low-cut tops, or other "sexy" styles. A woman who simply wants to be in style might buy and wear these clothes. She may want a man to admire her fashion sense—but that's a far cry from wanting him to have sex with her.

Of course, people's ideas about what's "sexy" varies. Some men get turned on when a woman shows a lot of skin; other men find it exciting when a woman covers herself up, so that they can imagine what might be underneath. Some men find certain colors or fabrics sexy, so that if a woman shows up in a red dress or a leather skirt they might see her as giving them a sexual message, even though for her red suggests independence and leather toughness.

There are also women who like to get men's attention and appreciation of their sexuality without being interested in acting on it. If you think about the stars Cher and Madonna, for example, you can see that they want their fans to have a certain response to them based on the clothes they wear and the image they present. That doesn't mean, however, that they are telling every one of their fans that they are interested in having sex with them! Even if Cher or Madonna showed up at, say, a private interview in one of their typical outfits, no one would assume that they were conveying that they wanted to have sex with the reporter. They would merely be trying to present a certain sexy image, separate from their particular decisions about when they felt like having sex.

Sometimes, too, girls don't know the message that they are giving out. A young, inexperienced girl might dress in a way that a boy finds sexy without realizing that she's doing it.

Of course, if a girl is a lesbian (a girl who is interested in sexual relationships with other girls), she might dress a certain way in order to be attractive—but to other women, not to men. A boy who believed that this girl was "asking for it" by the way she dressed would not be understanding her message correctly.

Some girls are survivors of sexual abuse. They were forced into sexual relationships when they were still children, often by members of their own family or family friends. They may still be in such relationships while they are teenagers. This kind of experience is particularly damaging because it teaches the child that *all* relationships can be sexual, and that sex is based on someone taking advantage of your weakness and inexperience.

A girl with this type of background may not know when she is dressing with a sexual message and when she isn't.

Or she may feel that she *must* present herself sexually, that she has no choice—even though she doesn't really want a sexual relationship. She may be giving out a message that says "I know I'm not good for anything except sex," or one that says, "Go ahead and try and have sex with me—at least I can say no to you, even if I couldn't say no to my father or my stepfather." Clearly, her dressing in a "sexy" way is not the same as her saying that she genuinely wants a sexual relationship with a particular guy.

As you can see, girls may dress in ways that guys find sexy for all sorts of reasons and in order to give out all sorts of messages. Whatever the circumstances, dressing a certain way is not the same as agreeing to sex. That's as foolish as saying that if a guy dresses up with expensive clothes and drives a nice car, he is saying that he wants to be robbed or have his car stolen. A man showing off that he has money does not mean that he wants someone else to force him to give up the money, just as a woman showing off her attractiveness does not mean that she wants someone to force her to have sex.

Myth: Guys have such strong sexual feelings that they can't control themselves—so it's up to girls to make sure that guys aren't tempted.

Fact: Both males and females have strong sexual feelings—and both males and females have the ability to control themselves. What would you think of someone who said, "It was the store's fault for letting me in the door—they should have known that once I saw all those great CDs, I wouldn't be able to resist shoplifting!" Sure, being in a store full of things you want might be tempting—but growing up means learning how to act according to your principles, not according to your impulses. Likewise, being with an attractive girl might be tempting to a boy, but if he's old enough to be sexually interested, he's old enough to act responsibly.

The idea of women tempting men is at least as old as the biblical story of Adam and Eve. According to that story, Adam is perfectly happy to obey God's law—until Eve picked the apple from the tree and held it out to him.

Somehow, Adam just "couldn't help himself"—and somehow, that was Eve's fault.

Many other stories, movies, plays, and television shows portray evil women tempting innocent men, often by "taking advantage" of the man's sexual desires. This is a powerful myth in our society—but it simply isn't true. Even if a woman does behave in this way, a man has the physical capacity to control his own sexual behavior. Except for the last few seconds before a man ejaculates, or comes, he is physically able to stop sexual activity at any time.

In fact, it's perfectly easy to imagine circumstances in which a man could control himself, even if he's almost ready to go "all the way." Say, for example, that a guy and a girl are just on the verge of having sex—and that guy's girlfriend walks into the room. Do you imagine that the guy could control himself under those circumstances? Or say that the intruder is his minister, priest, or rabbi—or his mother or father? Most likely, the man would be so unwilling to continue with such a private act in front of those people that he would easily be able to stop.

If this is so, then a man is also "physically" able to stop himself when a woman says no. All that's required is for him to feel that respecting her no is as important to him as protecting his own privacy. Making this decision is *his* responsibility, not the woman's. If she makes her wishes known, she should be able to assume that they will be respected.

Myth: A guy's sexual feelings are so powerful that if a girl doesn't give in to them, the guy could be physically damaged.

Fact: Both men and women have powerful sexual feelings—but neither sex can be physically damaged by sexual frustration. If a guy's feelings are not satisfied in any other way, he will probably have a "wet dream"—sexual release that comes when he is asleep.

The myth about men's powerful sexuality extends to the idea of "blue balls." When a man has been sexually excited or aroused for a long period of time without being able to come, his testicles (balls) become engorged with (full of) blood. The man experiences this as pressure and discomfort. However, the myth that the testicles will explode and the man will never be able to father children is just that—a myth. The worst that will happen is that the man will feel uncomfortable for a while. If he comes, the discomfort ends fairly quickly; if he doesn't, the discomfort ends somewhat more slowly.

Of course, there are many ways in which a man can deal with this discomfort that don't involve forcing a person to have sex. He might masturbate, so that he comes by himself. Or he can allow the pressure to relax by itself, over several hours. If he falls asleep in this condition, he might come during his sleep, having a "wet dream." In any case, he is in no physical danger whatsoever.

There are really two issues here. One is whether a man is in actual physical danger. The other, however, is whether the man has the right to use a woman to avoid discomfort. A guy might be insulted at being told to masturbate or have a wet dream, but being insulted is not the same thing as being in physical danger.

Once again, we turn to an analogy. Let's say you're stranded downtown around dinnertime and you don't have any money. No one can pick you up for a least four or five hours, and in the meantime, you're so hungry you think you can't stand it. Does this hunger give you the right to steal food? If you are a diabetic or have some other medical condition that might really place you in physical danger, perhaps it does. For most of us, however, going without a meal or two might present intense discomfort—but no real danger. Most of us would agree that a person who has missed only one meal does not have the right to steal from a restaurant or grocery store. Likewise, there is no danger associated with sexual frustration that gives a person the right to force his wishes on another.

Myth: If a girl starts being sexual with a guy, she has to go all the way; otherwise, she's "leading him on."

Fact: Both guys and girls have the right to explore sexually, to listen to their own feelings, to set limits, and to change their minds. A girl can say yes to kissing and no to petting, or yes to making out one night and then no to the same thing another night. This myth is like saying that if you lend your car to your friend to go on a quick errand downtown, he can assume that he's free to take it on a 500-mile trip into the mountains—otherwise, you've "led him on."

Of course, sometimes girls—and boys—do tease their dates, pretending to be available for more than they really are. And sometimes girls—and boys—use their sexual attractiveness to manipulate others. But if a guy feels frustrated with a girl's behavior in this regard, the solution is for him to talk about it with her or stop seeing her—not to force her into doing something that she really doesn't want to do. One person's teasing or manipulative behavior is no excuse for another person's violent crime.

As we have seen, a large percentage of men in all the studies cited above believed that if a woman "led a man on," that somehow justified his forcing her to have sex. Part of the problem with this way of thinking comes from confusion about the behavior that we call "leading a man on." Would that term include a woman's simply asking a man out? That would imply that the only reason a woman would ask a guy out was to have sex with him. But maybe the woman just wants to spend a pleasant evening talking or at the movies. Maybe she's lonely and just wants someone to pass the time with. Maybe she's interested in the guy but doesn't want to have sex right away—or maybe she limits all her sexual relationships to kissing and making out, deciding to wait to have intercourse until she's older. There are lots of reasons a woman might ask a man out that don't include having sexual intercourse, so why would asking a guy out seem like "leading him on?"

What about going back to the guy's apartment or house with him? Is that leading a guy on? Again, the woman might do this for many reasons. She might want to kiss the guy or make out with him but not to have sex with him. She might even think she wants to have sex but feel differently once she has started kissing or making out.

Does "leading on" include kissing a guy passionately? A man might believe that a woman would never let him know how turned on she was unless she really wanted to have sex. But of course, a woman might simply enjoy kissing and want to stop there. Or she might really be turned on but decide not to have sex for all sorts of reasons—it might be against her principles, she might be afraid of pregnancy or sexually transmitted disease, she might feel that she isn't emotionally ready for a sexual relationship with this guy even though she feels very turned on. In all of these cases, the woman is simply showing that she is turned on by kissing—she is not necessarily intentionally giving the man the message that she is ready for sex.

Of course, a man who wants sex and thinks he is going to have it might be frustrated when he finds out the disappointing truth—but that doesn't necessarily mean that the *woman* wanted him to believe he was going to have sex. That might simply have been his own interpretation of events. Likewise, a woman who wants sex with a man might be frustrated if she doesn't get what she wants—but that doesn't give her the right to pressure or force him to "put out" for her.

Part of the problem is that in our society, actions that mean one thing to a woman might mean something very different to a man. She may just be trying to get to know the man better, or want a romantic relationship that includes kissing or making out but nothing more. But if he sees her actions as promises of sex, he may feel that by not having sex with him, the woman is breaking a promise.

Sometimes the reverse is true: The woman feels that the man has made a promise to her, even though the couple hasn't actually spoken about their relationship. The woman might feel that the man "owes" her sex or a romantic relationship. Or, more often, she might feel that by having sex with her, the man owes her something else—love, commitment, being faithful, or an ongoing relationship that will last as long as the woman is willing to keep having sex.

In fact, actions don't constitute promises. It's true that in our society, certain actions might imply a certain future. A girl who agrees to park with a guy in a secluded spot may be implying some agreement to some kind of sexual activity—kissing or making out if not intercourse. A guy who takes a girl out three nights in a row seems to be giving her the message that he's very interested in her and he won't just disappear after the third date.

However, even in these cases, if the person hasn't told you specifically that he or she agrees to a particular kind of relationship, you can't really assume that they've interpreted their actions in the same way that you have. Maybe the girl is going to the secluded spot because she likes nature or because she wants to talk privately. Maybe the guy is seeing the girl three nights in a row because those are the nights his girlfriend is out of town. Certainly the girl's actions don't give the guy the right to force the girl into having sex, any more than the guy's actions give the girl the right to force the guy into a committed relationship.

A person who behaves in a certain way and then doesn't follow through may not be a very nice person. He or she may in fact be leading another person on, deliberately or accidentally. A person who leads others on may do so out of a desire to feel powerful, to get revenge, or to prove something about himself or herself. Or the "leader-on" may be innocent or irresponsible, not aware of the effect that certain actions are having on others or not concerned with other people's feelings.

Many women do use their sexuality as a kind of weapon against men, often because they feel so powerless that they consider that to be the only way they can get what they want in a male-female relationship. We don't think this is good behavior—but it doesn't justify forcing a woman into something she really doesn't want. Even if a woman does deliberately lead a man to think he's going to have sex with her and then does not come through, that doesn't give the man the right to force sex on her, any more than a woman has the right to force a man into a committed, monogamous relationship. The difference, of course, is that the man can use his physical power to force sex on a woman, whereas a woman has no comparable way of forcing what she wants onto a man.

If a woman does lead a man on, that may give the man the right to be angry with her or to call her a manipulative person. He may not want to spend any more time with a person who behaves in this frustrating or manipulative way, intentionally or unintentionally. But however angry or hurt or disappointed he may be, he is still not justified in raping the woman.

We'll end with one final analogy about "leading on." Let's say you go into a restaurant and start chatting with the owner, who is also the waiter. You tell the owner that you love desserts and you can hardly wait to get to the end of the meal so you can order dessert. You ask the owner about what kinds of desserts he offers, and throughout the meal, you keep reminding him that you plan to order dessert. When you finish eating your main course, you ask to see the dessert menu. Then you ask the owner to bring the desserts from the kitchen so you can get a better look at them. You spend 10 minutes asking detailed questions about what each dessert is and how it's made. At the end of all this, you say, "You know, I'm really not that hungry any more. I think I'll just have coffee."

Have you led the owner on? Probably. Is the owner frustrated, angry, and disappointed? Almost certainly. Does the owner have the right to bring out a dessert, hold a gun to your head, force you to eat dessert and then put it on your bill? Absolutely not.

Myth: If a woman asks a man out, she's probably promiscuous and is asking for sex.

Fact: If a woman asks a man out, she wants to go out with him. You can't draw any further conclusions about her past sexual history or about her sexual intentions from the mere fact that she asked a guy out on a date.

Ironically, many of the other circumstances that we've talked about where men feel justified in forcing sex on a woman have to do with the woman's being passive. Perhaps by going along with the man's wishes earlier in the evening, the woman has given the impression that she'll allow the man to have his way sexually, as well. Perhaps by allowing the man to be "in the driver's seat" or to pay for the evening, the woman has put herself in a position where it may be more difficult to say no to sex.

We might think, however, that when the woman takes the reins and asks for a date, she would not be making herself more vulnerable to the possibility of getting raped. Unfortunately, as shown by the survey conducted at Texas A&M and Indiana Universities, many men interpret a woman's asking them out as evidence that she is "easy" sexually and that they are therefore justified in forcing her to have sex. Even though a woman who asks a guy out is not fitting the traditional "sex-object" passive stereotype and even though she is demonstrating by her actions that she has a mind of her own and a willingness to take some of the responsibility for the date, the men in the survey still felt they would be justified in forcing her to have sex. Why?

To us, this seems like an extension of the "good girl/bad girl" stereotype. Since good girls are supposed to be passive, waiting for the man to make up *his* mind, an active woman must be a bad girl. Who else would ask a man out on a date but a woman who is eager or desperate for sex? And if a man believes that a woman is willing to have sex and then finds out that she's not, doesn't he then have the "right" to get by force what he thought he was going to get by consent?

Of course, you can see the flaws in this way of thinking. There are many reasons a girl might ask a guy out. She might want to have sex with him—or she might just want to get to know him better. She might be interested in a romantic relationship—or she might decide at the end of the evening that this guy is not for her. Either way, sex is her decision as well as her date's. If you think that a girl who asks a guy out on a date is asking to have forced sex, you might just as well say that a store that entices you to its grand opening with free samples and big sales is inviting you to help yourself to its other merchandise. The store *does* want you to take the free samples and it *does* offer some merchandise at sale prices. It *doesn't* want you to help yourself to anything you feel like. By the same token, the woman who asks a man out *does* want him to accept the date. She *may* even want him to kiss her or to make out. If she decides to, she *might* want to have sex with him. But what she *doesn't* want is for the man to feel he has the right to help himself to whatever he wants, regardless of what she has offered.

Myth: Once a woman says she's going to have sex with a man, she can't really change her mind. That is, it doesn't count as rape if the woman said yes, then changed her mind and said no.

Fact: A woman has the right to change her mind at any point—and a man never has the right to force her, based on the things she has said in the past. Once again, a man may get angry, frustrated, or disappointed by a woman's changing her mind, and he may want to express those feelings to her. That's not the same as forcing her to stick to her original decision, however.

An analogy makes this clear. Say you decide to lend your friend your car and then change your mind. Would it be all right for your friend to take your car anyway? Let's say you've gone so far as to watch your friend get into the driver's seat, start up the engine, and put the car into drive. Suddenly, you rush up to your friend and say, "Stop! I've changed my mind! you can't take my car after all!" Would your friend have the right to ignore your wishes and drive the car away?

We don't think so—and the law would agree. If your friend takes your car even after you've explicitly said no, that's car theft. If a man forces a woman into sex after she's explicitly said no, that's rape. The fact that the no used to be yes has nothing to do with it. In fact, if you had a car phone and you called your friend on the phone after he or she was already halfway to the destination, you would still legally have the right to insist that the car be brought back. After all, it's your car. And, in the case of sex, it's the woman's body. She has the right to change her mind at any time she wants.

Of course, you might not be showing very good judgment by waiting until your car is in drive to change your mind.

First of all, your friend is almost sure to get angry. Second, by then he or she has the *power* to drive away against your wishes, even if he or she doesn't have the *right*. A woman might not be showing good judgment by waiting too long to say no for she may find it physically more difficult to get the man to stop. However, you have the right to assume that your friend is not a thief, and a woman has the right to assume that her date is not a rapist. Might does not make right, even if it does allow a person to get his way.

Myth: Most so-called cases of date rape happen when a woman willingly has sex—and then changes her mind *afterward*.

Fact: Frequently, women give men all sorts of signals that mean no *before* the sexual act takes place. However, if a man doesn't take a woman's no seriously or if he believes that women like to be forced, he won't realize that a woman has been saying no—until afterward. Then it may seem to him that she has changed her mind, when she has really been saying no all along.

How does this happen? Sometimes it's a case of genuine misunderstanding. Because communication between men and women about sex is so difficult, because men believe so many myths about what a woman's actions mean, and because women are so often not good at saying no in a clear way, men may not realize that a woman has been saying no all along.

Suppose a woman says no in a playful way. She may be trying to make a joke out of it so that the man won't get angry—but to him, it may look like flirting. Suppose a woman pushes a man's hand away without saying anything. She may feel so ashamed or scared that she can't speak—but to him, it may look like she simply wants his hand somewhere else, not that she is specifically saying no to sex.

Then, afterward, when it's all over, if the woman cries, or accuses him of rape, the man may be genuinely shocked. To him, it may seem as though she really did say yes, and she is only now feeling bad about what she did. In fact, to her, it seemed as though she had been saying no all along but the

still hold that person responsible. For example, if a boy killed the neighbor's dog while he was drunk, would you say, "He didn't really mean it, it was the liquor?" Or would you say, "That's the kind of act that is wrong whether the person is drunk or sober?"

You might recall that we said earlier that a man has no right to take advantage of a woman's being drunk or high to get her to have sex with him. At first glance, this argument might seem to contradict what we just said above. If the man is responsible for his actions while he is drunk, why isn't the woman equally responsible for hers?

Of course, women are just as responsible as men for their actions while drunk or high, and a woman has no right to try to get a man drunk to force him into a position where he can't say no to her. Nor does a woman have the right to use her own drunkenness or state of being high as an excuse for forcing a man into a sexual relationship.

When the person who is *being* forced is drunk or high, however, that's a different story. In that case, he or she is not using an altered state as an excuse for hurting *someone else*. Instead, the altered state is making it more difficult for the person to exercise good judgment and self-protection.

Perhaps a person shouldn't get into that state while on a date. (We'll talk more about these kinds of issues in chapter 5.) Nevertheless, using poor judgment about yourself isn't the same as taking advantage of somebody else. Suppose a person gets so drunk that he tries to give his wallet away to a stranger, or suppose a person is so high that she doesn't even notice that a stranger is robbing her. Clearly, this person is not showing good judgment by allowing drugs or alcohol to put him or her into such a vulnerable state. Nevertheless, the person who takes the wallet is clearly taking unfair advantage of the drunk or stoned person. That person's bad behavior isn't excused by the other person's poor judgment. And if the person taking the wallet helped get the other person drunk or high in order to have an easier time with the robbery, the behavior is even worse.

Getting drunk and losing a wallet may show poor judgment and self-destructive behavior, but you couldn't really say that the person *wanted* to lose his money—it was just the consequence of a poor decision. Likewise, a woman who gets so drunk or high on a date that she can't genuinely say no to sex may have shown poor judgment, but that doesn't mean she deserves to be raped or that she wanted that bad consequence to happen. She is responsible for her poor decision—but the man is responsible for the rape.

On the other hand, getting drunk and shooting the neighbor's dog is a crime. Whatever the person wanted or didn't want, the dog is dead: The crime has been committed. Getting drunk is no excuse for committing a crime—and date rape is a crime.

Looking at the "Gray Areas": Rape Versus Sexual Aggression

As you can see from the discussion in this chapter, there are a lot of "gray areas" as we look at date rape. We have said that if a man threatens to hurt a woman unless she has sex, it's rape. But what if he simply calls her names or threatens to spread rumors about her? We've said that a man might use physical pressure to force a woman to have sex, either by literally forcing her, by threatening to hurt her, or by threatening to leave her stranded. But what if he uses emotional pressure, claiming that he'll stop going out with her if she doesn't have sex with him, or saying that she's not a "real woman" if she can't satisfy him?

Various experts on date rape disagree about exact definitions. In our opinion, forced sex is rape only when physical force is used, when there's the overt or covert threat of physical force, when there's some other type of coercion—such as leaving a person stranded—or when the rape target is made incapable of making a real decision by drink, drugs, sleep, or some other condition. Other types of pressure—threats to spread rumors or to break up; insults, coaxing, etc.—are emotional, not physical. In our opinion, they constitute sexual aggression, not rape.

We make this distinction not because rape is serious and sexual aggression is not. We think they're both serious. Rather we make the distinction because a girl has a different set of choices in each case. Because each type of action is a different kind of threat, each requires a different set of defenses.

We'll talk more about how to protect oneself against date rape in chapter 5. For now, we want to point out that our definition of rape is that the woman has no choice, or at best, very little choice. She may not be physically capable of preventing the man from forcing sex, like Alicia, who was forced by Luis to have sex at a drinking party. Or the woman may believe that she's physically not capable of preventing the man from forcing her into sex—for example, the case of Lou Ellen, who, stranded at the lake with Bill, knew she needed Bill to get home and also believed that if she tried to hit Bill, he'd hit her harder.

With sexual aggression, on the other hand, the choices may be painful or difficult, but they are somewhat broader. It may not be pleasant to have a man spread rumors about you—but a woman has a choice about whether she would rather be the target of rumors or of sexual assault. In rape, the woman has no choice—she is physically forced against her will or forced because she believes that her survival is at stake.

Likewise, it may be painful to face losing a relationship, but a man who threatens to leave you if you don't do what he wants is not the same as a man who threatens to hit you if you don't do what he wants. In one case, you're risking being alone—in another case, you're risking your life or your safety.

Of course, neither kind of behavior reflects very well on the man involved. Whether a man is guilty of rape or sexual aggression, he is still trying to force someone else to go along with him rather than trying to work things out respectfully with an equal partner. Both kinds of behavior are painful and upsetting to the woman involved. Both rape and sexual aggression give women the message that they don't count, that men feel free to use them as objects, that they don't have enough power in the world to get what they want. Both kinds of actions make it difficult for men and women to get along, for both sexes to trust each other and be sexually open with each other.

What About Flirting: Does No Ever Mean Yes?

As we saw earlier, there is a myth that says that a date rape is a date where the woman had sex and then changed her mind afterward. Although this may happen occasionally, we think it's much more common for the woman to have been saying no all along but that her message wasn't clear to the man. Then, afterward when the woman cries or is upset, the man believes that she simply changed her mind, rather than seeing that she had been saying no earlier, as well.

This myth has its roots in another myth, one that claims that sexually eager women need to pretend that they "don't really want it." That way, afterward, they don't have to feel guilty. This goes back to the idea that "nice girls" aren't supposed to like sex, so that a girl must pretend she doesn't like sex in order to seem like a nice girl.

In fact, there is probably good reason to be confused in this area, because many girls *do* give guys mixed messages about having sex. Some girls do feel guilty about having sex, or a girl might believe that guys will look down on her or consider her a "slut" if she shows that she enjoys sex. Such girls may expect a guy to understand when no means yes and when it really means no.

Another area of confusion comes from some girls' unwillingness to hurt guys' feelings. Compare the statements in the following list with those in the second. Which statements seem clearer and easier to understand? Which seem more polite? Which seem more like the kind a girl might really make on a date, especially if she really likes a guy and wants to keep going out with him?

"I want to, but I don't think we should."
"Don't do that right now."
"Maybe we'd better not do this."
"This is really great—but it's late and I have to go."

"Look, I want to kiss you but I don't want you to touch my breasts."
"I like making out, but I don't want to go all the way."
"I'm not ready for sex, and I don't know when I will be ready. Don't plan on having sex with me any time in the near future."
"I really don't want you to do that."

A guy might feel that the statements in the first list are not really nos. If a girl says, "I want to, but I don't think we should," he might think she means that his job is to convince her that they should in order to take all the blame on himself. If she says, "Don't do that right now," he might think she wants to do it later. If she says, "Maybe we'd better not do this," he might think she's counting on him to be a take-charge guy and say, "Oh yes, I think we should" or a protective man, saying, "Don't worry, it'll be okay." And of course, putting the no in terms of being late certainly sounds like a promise for the next time, when the sexual activity might start earlier.

We think that one of the ways to stop date rape is for girls to be clearer about when they really are saying no; and we'll give some suggestions for how to do this in chapter 5. On the other hand, we also think boys need to take more responsibility in making sure they really are hearing what their partners are saying. That way, boys can be sure that they are not guilty of date rape. We have to conclude that just because no occasionally does mean yes, that doesn't mean that a guy has the right to act on that. It's safer to believe a girl means no when she says no than to assume that she just needs to be pushed a little before she gives in. It's safer still to ask a girl what she means and to make sure that she really has given her consent.

When Boys Are the Target

As we have seen, date rape involves the use of physical force, the threat of physical force, or manipulation of some other kind of physical incapacity (such as being drunk or stoned, or being too young to make good decisions) to make another person have sex. Sexual aggression involves the use of emotional pressure such as mockery, insults, hurt feelings, threats of spreading rumors, or threats of breaking up. Both date rape and sexual aggression are harmful acts, because both involve pushing a person into something he or she doesn't really want.

Many people believe that women are not physically capable of raping men. In fact, a girl might use a weapon, a situation (such as controlling a boy's access to transportation home), or even her own physical strength to force a boy into sex. Usually, a man does not become erect (hard) unless he himself is sexually aroused, but in some cases, fear can produce an erection (a hard-on). A man who is genuinely afraid of being hurt by a woman could become erect enough to have sex with her.

Of course, in our society women rarely use physical force to coerce men into sex, even though this would theoretically be possible. Most women are not as physically strong as most men, but women could equalize the situation by carrying weapons, learning a martial art or setting up situations in which they have physical control—if they were interested in forcing men into sex. As we have seen, however, the way our society constructs sex roles, this is not an option that fits most women's ideas of what they need to be a "real woman." The image of a real man as a take-charge guy, coupled with the image of women as sex objects or as somehow worth less than men helps support the idea of a man's raping a woman. There are no corresponding images that help support the idea of a woman's using actual force to get her way with a man.

However, there is a great deal of support in our current sex roles for sexual aggression. Both women and men may buy into the idea that guys are ready for sex all the time. Thus a woman might feel justified in demanding that a guy "put out" for her and might feel further justified in using emotional—if not physical—ways of forcing him to do it. Just as a man who committed date rape might not realize that he had actually forced a woman into a painful act, a woman who committed sexual aggression might not realize that she has in fact caused a man pain.

Likewise, a guy who believes that he is *supposed* to be ready for sex with any woman, at any time, might not realize the extent to which he feels pain, anger, and helplessness at having been pushed into a sexual situation that he really didn't want. With the current attitude toward "scoring," it is almost impossible in our society for a guy to say, even to himself, "I want to kiss this girl but not make out with her," or "I'm not ready for sex yet," or "I want to take things more slowly."

This type of difficulty could affect a guy in two ways. First, it might keep him from taking care of himself, from standing up to a woman's sexual aggression in a way that he'll feel good about afterward. After all, if he's supposed to want sex all the time, why wouldn't he go along with a "willing" woman, especially if she is taunting him about being a "real" man or threatening to tell people that he's gay?

Second, after the sexual aggression is over, a guy might have a very difficult time realizing what has happened to him. Since our cultural stereotypes are so strong, many people, both men and women, don't even recognize the possibility that a "weak" woman could force a "strong" man into an unwanted sexual act. And if the guy is supposed to like sex all the time, he has no basis for feeling used, helpless, or hurt.

Ironically, many of the myths that support men's raping of women might also support women's using sexual aggression against men. The idea that someone who "leads you on" deserves to be forced into sex is one that many women may also buy into. Thus if a guy is sexual or flirtatious with them, they may feel that he owes them something more, something that they are justified in pressuring him into if he isn't already willing. Likewise, if a woman asks a man out on a date or pays for him, she may feel that her generosity gives her the same "rights" that a man would have in the same situation—the "right" to demand sex in return for paying.

Men, too, may believe in these myths even when they, not women, are the targets. Once again, we see that the system of inequality between men and women ends up hurting both men and women. Men's and women's roles are set up in ways that often cause pain, whether the roles are traditional or reversed.

4

What Is Acquaintance Rape?

Just as it's hard to define date rape because of the confusion surrounding that issue, so is it hard to define acquaintance rape. Although most people can agree that a sudden attack by a stranger counts as rape, what should we make of a rape between two people who have known each other for a long time, or between two people who seem to have been talking pleasantly or otherwise enjoying each other's company before the rape occurred? After all, most people don't let robbers or murderers into their homes—how is it possible that a woman might willingly invite a rapist into her house? Most people know whether their friends and acquaintances are thieves or violent criminals—how is it possible that a woman could be acquainted with a rapist without knowing it?

The Legal Definition of Rape

In most states, the legal definition of rape involves a woman being forced into sexual intercourse with a man against her will. Forcing a woman to commit or to submit to oral sex (penis to mouth or mouth to vagina) or to anal sex (penis to anus [rear opening]) is also considered rape in most states. In many states, rape is also considered to have taken place if the woman is so far "under the influence" (drunk or high) that she cannot make a good decision, as well as if the woman is asleep, mentally incompetent, or too young to understand what she is agreeing to.

In theory, these legal definitions hold good whether the rapist is a stranger, an acquaintance, or someone that the woman was out with on a date. However, in fact, many people have a much more difficult time accepting that a rape has occurred if the rapist is someone the woman knows. Women themselves may not see a sexual attack by an acquaintance as rape. Why is acquaintance rape so difficult to recognize?

Recognizing Acquaintance Rape

We might expect that acquaintance rape would be easier to recognize than date rape. Frequently, in a date-rape trial, the accused will freely admit that sex took place—he will simply insist that the sex didn't count as rape. In non-dating situations, we don't usually expect sex to occur. Yet even in those situations, a man might claim that the woman or girl was willing. Remember the example of Lydia, at the beginning of the book? She let a family friend into her apartment, he raped her, and afterward he threatened to tell her family that she had seduced him. If the meter man were to be caught, he might also claim, sincerely or not, that he believed Ellen was interested in having sex with him.

Take a look at the following scenarios. What do they tell us about how acquaintance rape might occur and why it might be hard to recognize?

Melissa has known Johnny for a couple of years at school. When the teacher assigns them to a history project together, the two of them make plans to go to his house to study one afternoon after school. Melissa believes Johnny's family will be home, but she realizes, after she's been there for an hour, that everyone else has left. Johnny starts talking about how much he's always liked her, which makes Melissa very uncomfortable. Still, she doesn't want to hurt his feelings. She says, "Oh, yes, I like you, too." When Johnny puts his arms around her and starts kissing her, Melissa tries to push him away, but gently, so she won't hurt his feelings. After all, she has to go on seeing him in school. Johnny says, "You said you liked me—and you came over to my house to be alone with me. I know you want this as much as I do." Melissa is so embarrassed and upset that she doesn't know what to do. She doesn't like the idea of hitting or kicking Johnny—she really doesn't want to physically hurt anybody. She's also afraid that if she does fight back, Johnny will hurt her. And she's afraid that even if Johnny's parents do come home, they will somehow blame her. Johnny is able to force her to have sex with him, but Melissa still can't figure out what she did wrong to make this happen.

Patrice likes visiting the pottery store in her neighborhood. The guy who owns the store is always happy to see her, and if it's not too busy, he'll tell her about the different people who make the beautiful bowls and pitchers that he sells. One Saturday morning, she stops by the store and no other customer is there. The owner asks if she would like to see a new shipment that just came in, which is stored in the basement. Patrice happily agrees. The owner leaves his clerk in charge of the store to take Patrice downstairs. While she is looking at the pottery, he comes up behind her and puts his hands on her breasts. At first, she is so surprised that she doesn't know what to do. She tries just pushing him away without saying anything, as if she could just pretend that nothing bad was happening, but he holds her tighter and presses himself against her. Patrice tries to get away, but she thinks, "If I break any of the pottery here, he'll make me pay for it. And if I scream, then the clerk will know what's happening—I don't want him to know! Besides, this guy is his boss. That clerk might not even help me—he might even help his boss. And if my parents find out, they'll blame me for coming down here in the first place. How could I have been so stupid?"

In both cases, the girls are having a hard time recognizing their situations as rape because they didn't expect to be attacked. They are dealing with acquaintances, men or boys that they have known for a while. They are also dealing with situations—a family home, a public store—where they have felt safe in the past and might expect to feel safe again. Melissa would never go to a guy's house late at night on a date—but she thought it was safe to go to Johnny's house after school to study. Patrice would never go into a bar on a Saturday night—but she thought it was safe to go into a store on a Saturday morning.

Rather than recognizing what is happening to them as rape, the girls expect others to blame them for their situation. Melissa thinks that her family and Johnny's family will hold her responsible, not Johnny. Patrice expects that the clerk will be on his boss's side, not hers, and she worries that her family will blame her for showing poor judgment rather than blaming the store owner for committing a crime.

Because the girls have trouble seeing what is going on as rape, they feel uncomfortable about fighting back. Melissa worries about injuring Johnny. Patrice worries about breaking the owner's pottery. Both girls worry about not being strong enough to fight back, about getting hurt in addition to being forced into sexual behavior. And both girls feel deeply ashamed and uncomfortable because what they thought was a pleasant safe situation has turned into a dangerous and threatening one.

The sad thing about both of these situations is that they show how blurry the line can be between men who are trustworthy and men who are not. Melissa had agreed to study history with Johnny, not to go out on a date with him. She had no reason to think that he expected sex from her, let alone that he would under any circumstances force her into doing anything that she didn't want to do. Patrice went into the store to look at the pottery. She had no reason to think that the friendly man who liked to chat with her would turn out to be a threatening person who would attack her.

To us, these stories raise a lot of painful questions. Should girls *always* expect to be attacked, in order to protect themselves from acquaintance rape? Is it *ever* all right for a woman to be alone with a man? If an acquaintance rapist can seem like a nice, ordinary person, can a woman *ever* tell which men are dangerous and which men are safe?

The Dilemma of Acquaintance Rape

These painful questions make it difficult for many people to think clearly about acquaintance rape. It is very uncomfortable to realize that, in one sense, any man might choose to commit rape even if in fact *most* men don't. We do not assume, for example, that if we invite a family friend over for dinner, he will end up stealing the silver or threatening us with murder. Sadly, it's far more possible that such a friend would commit the crime of rape. Likewise, in the example of Ellen and the meter reader, Ellen's family trusted this man not to rob or assault them when they let him in the house. But the man could not be trusted not to rape.

In a way, society *has* accepted the possibility that any man could be a rapist. That's why girls are told from an early age not to go places alone, not to be out alone after dark, not to dress in certain ways, and not to invite men into their homes. That's why, until fairly recently, girls were not allowed out alone with guys on dates. The implication was that girls had to protect themselves against the possibility of rape by staying in crowded, well-lighted places, by never being alone with a man under any circumstances, by not dressing in ways that acknowledged their own sexual feelings.

However, this is a kind of backward way of addressing the possibility of date or acquaintance rape. Instead of condemning a system in which a man feels able to rape women, society's rules suggest that there is something wrong with a *woman* who has not properly protected herself. Instead of asking why an otherwise nice and law-abiding man feels entitled to commit a crime, some people would rather believe that it is the woman who behaves badly—that she somehow "makes" the crime happen.

As we've said, given the circumstances in our society, girls and women *do* have to protect themselves against rape. There is such a thing as foolish or risky behavior, which girls and women (and, often, boys and men) should avoid. However, acting foolishly is not the same thing as committing a crime. Leaving your house unlocked is not the same thing as committing a robbery.

To get back to the painful questions we raised a little earlier, we think that, unfortunately, there are no simple answers. We don't believe that girls and women should move through the world with fear and mistrust, seeing a possibility of attack in every encounter. That's no way to live!

Besides, it cuts off many pleasant possibilities of working or chatting with men in non-sexual situations.

On the other hand, acquaintance rape does exist, and we can't pretend it doesn't. In a sense, women and girls have to have a kind of double vision, believing both in their own safety and in the possibility of being attacked.

One way of coping with this dilemma is being very clear about when rape has occurred, and recognizing that the man, not the woman is to blame for it. If both Melissa and Patrice had felt confident that they had done nothing wrong, that the blame lay with their attackers, they might have felt more comfortable with defending themselves. Melissa might not have worried about hurting Johnny—after all, he was hurting her. Patrice might not have worried about breaking the owner's pottery—after all, he was injuring her. Both girls might have been angry, rather than ashamed, that the males they were with had taken advantage of a pleasant relationship to stage an attack.

Another way of coping with this dilemma is believing in your right to protect yourself and expanding your ability to do so. Girls and women who have taken self-defense classes, for example, say that in general, they face the world with more confidence knowing that they have the physical strength and skill to defend themselves in case of an attack. Believing in your right to speak up if something feels wrong to you or to tell someone to stop it instead of worrying about hurting his feelings is a way of finding safety inside yourself, even if other people sometimes can't be trusted.

Once again, we want to emphasize that there are no simple answers. A woman might believe in her right to protect herself, she might know whom to blame, she might even have a black belt in karate—and she might still be vulnerable to acquaintance rape. The dilemma of acquaintance rape means that girls and women have to make their own decisions about how to protect themselves, while knowing that there are no foolproof solutions that guarantee protection.

Group Rape

Most of the time, when we hear the words *acquaintance rape* or *date rape* we assume that only two people are involved—the two people who are acquainted or the two people who go on a date. Sometimes, however, a group of people might be involved in a rape. These experiences can be even more upsetting to a woman because they give the message that she is facing not just betrayal by one man but hostility from a whole group of men, all of whom have agreed to support each other and to attack her or to allow her to be attacked.

One form of group rape occurs when more than one guy rapes the same woman. At a fraternity house party, for example, a woman might be forced into sex with several men, with the other men either watching or waiting nearby for "their turn." Even when guys are still living with their parents, they might arrange a party at which such group rapes take place.

Another form of group rape involves only one man actually having sex with the woman, but several other men helping him set up the conditions in which he can force sex on her. At a party, for example, several guys could cooperate in getting a woman drunk, refusing to give her a ride home, directing her onto a guy's bedroom, or even physically preventing her from leaving until the guy has been able to force her to have sex. Even though only one man is involved in the sexual part of the rape, several men are involved in forcing the woman into sex.

Sometimes the group involved is even more passive. The movie *The Accused*, for example, is based on an incident that took place several years ago, in which a woman was raped in a bar while other men looked on, refusing to come to her aid. Although the men had not participated in setting up the conditions for the rape, they ultimately supported the crime by cheering the man on and refusing to help the woman resist his physical force.

As we have seen, men who have committed date rape frequently don't even realize that they have forced a woman into doing something that she didn't want to do. They may genuinely believe that they were correctly reading her nos as yeses, or that the woman would be grateful afterward, once the man had "taken charge." In the case of group rape, however, every man involved must realize that the woman is being forced into a sexual act against her will. It is a measure of how difficult our society makes it to see women as equals, and of how much we still value the idea that "might makes right" that otherwise law-abiding and respect-ful men could join forces to commit such a painful and damaging crime.

5

Can It
Happen to Me?

So far, we've focused on defining what date and acquaintance rape are. We've also pointed out that the person
who commits the rape is the one responsible for it. The same
is true of sexual aggression. Unfortunately, there is a tendency in our society to "blame the victim"—to try to blame
the woman or man who was the target of a sexual attack by
saying that she or he was "provocative," "should have
known better," or was somehow "asking for it." Even if a
person shows bad judgment by, say, wearing an expensive
watch in a crime-ridden neighborhood, no one says that the
person "deserved" to be robbed by showing such poor
judgment, or that the person secretly "wanted" to be robbed,
or rashly "provoked" the robber by displaying wealth.

However, we might say that while the robbers are responsible for their own crime, there are steps that people can take
to protect themselves from being the victim of a crime. The
same is true of rape and sexual aggression. In this chapter,
we'll talk about what women can do to protect themselves.

Because many men commit date rape without even being aware of it, we'll also talk about how men can help make sure that they are not accidentally guilty of this crime. In the chapter's second-to-last section, we'll talk about ways in which both men and women can make sure that men are not the targets of sexual aggression from women.

Talking It Out

One of the greatest contributors to date rape is poor communication about sexual and romantic activity. To some extent this poor communication comes from the fact that in our society, men and women are faced with very different expectations about sex, dating, and relationships.

Men tend to be under a lot of pressure to "score," and they receive support for the belief that they "deserve" to be surrounded by sexy, adoring women who will do anything they desire. Meanwhile, they are supposed to act like "take-charge" guys while bearing all of the responsibility for asking girls out and paying for the date.

Women, on the other hand, are under a lot of pressure to have high-status or well-off boyfriends or husbands, and they receive support for the belief that they "deserve" to have a man take care of them. Meanwhile, they are supposed to act sexy and make themselves look attractive while still behaving like "good girls," or at least preserving a good reputation.

Because they have such different assumptions about what they want and what they deserve, men and women can often use the same words to mean quite different things. This frequently leads to a lot of confusion. Take a look at the following scenarios:

Jenna says to Mark, "I'm not ready for a serious relationship yet—can we just get to know each other first?" She means "I hope we can go steady soon, but I'm not ready to do it now. However, I'll still be upset if I think you're seeing other people—and I'll really be upset if I think you're having sex with other people. I have no idea when I'll be ready to have sex with you, or even if I'll ever want to."

Mark hears, "Maybe I'll be ready to have sex with you on our next date, or on the one after that. Meanwhile, since we're not 'serious', I assume you'll keep seeing other people."

Efraim says, "I really like you, and I want to get to know you better." He means, "I'd like to spend time with you that includes having sex. I'm not really thinking past the next date or two."

Marta thinks, "Oh, he *really* likes me. That means he really cares about me. Maybe we'll go steady soon, or even get engaged. He wants to 'get to know me better'— that means we'll be going out together for at least six months or so!"

Can you think of other examples of male-female miscommunication?

As you can see, the pressure on men to think about having sex and the pressure on women to think about forming long-term relationships help each gender distort what they hear. A man might think he has been clear with a woman, only to find out later that she was sure his words meant something completely different. Likewise, a woman might think she has clearly informed a man about what she wants and what she doesn't want, only to realize that he gives her words a very different meaning than she does.

Where date rape comes in is when men feel that they have been promised or offered sex. Frequently, date rape doesn't take place because the man plans to rape the woman. Rather, it may happen because the man plans to have sex. Then, when the woman isn't willing, the man feels justified in forcing her. The man may have been so sure that they were going to have sex that he doesn't even realize that he *is* forcing her.

Of course, the miscommunication that leads to date rape usually continues all the way through a date. For example, consider the following scenarios:

Jenna tells Mark, "That feels good, but I think we should stop." She means, "I think we've gone too far (*I think we should stop*)." He hears, "I like this and I don't really want to stop (*That feels good . . . we should stop* [but I don't really want to!])."

Luis tells Alicia, "I won't do anything you don't want me to." He means, "If I do something and you don't take my hand away or put up a big fight, you must want me to do it." She hears, "He can read my mind and he knows what I want, so nothing bad is going to happen. All I have to do is feel upset and he'll know it and stop."

As we saw in the last chapter, girls are brought up to be polite and to avoid hurting people's feelings, whereas guys are brought up to be assertive and determined about getting what they want. A girl might imagine that if she says bluntly, "Stop!" or, "I don't like that!" she'll hurt a guy's feelings. So she might soften her message by saying, "That feels good, but . . ." or, "Not right now, okay?"

In addition, girls often soften their sentences by ending them with questions, demonstrating that they want to get the other person's agreement. A guy who is intent on getting what he wants might mishear a girl's polite question—"Let's not do this, *okay?*"—as a genuine opening for him to offer another opinion—"No, it's not okay! I want to do this now." The girl is trying to give a definite message, but her way of talking and the guy's way of hearing encourage the guy to hear her definite no as an open-ended maybe that the guy can change into a yes if only he is persistent enough.

Under these circumstances, a guy might figure that if he just charges on and does what he wants, the girl will come around. He may also believe that he's supposed to know what a girl wants without asking, that asking somehow shows him up as a bad lover or an inexperienced man. He may be afraid that if he hesitates, acts unsure, or asks a question ("Do you like this?" "Should I keep touching you here?" "Do you want me to go further?") the girl will not respect him or will be angry with him for not knowing automatically what she wants.

None of these attitudes is helpful to good communication. The girl isn't saying clearly what she wants and how she feels. The guy isn't listening to what he's being told or asking for clarification.

What's the solution? We think that in general, girls need to become better at giving out clear, unmistakable messages, while, also in general, guys need to become better at listening and hearing messages accurately, and at asking for more information if they're not sure what the message is.

Following are two sets of lists. The first contains examples of unclear communication—things that a girl might say and the ways that a guy might misunderstand her. The second contains examples of clear communication—statements that can be clearly understood. Of course, both sets of lists might apply to the other sex if a guy is the target of sexual aggression by a girl.

Unclear Communication

- "Not right now, okay?"—The guy might think, "Okay, how about later?" or "No, it's not okay, and if I show her that it's not okay, she'll go along with me."
- "I really like this, but I don't think we should do it."—The guy might hear that she likes it, not that she doesn't want to do it. By saying that she doesn't think she "should" do it, the girl might seem to be asking the guy to take the responsibility for her doing it, since if she's a "good girl," she isn't supposed to want or like sex. The guy might think he's doing her a favor by forcing her to do something she "really likes" but doesn't think she "should" do.

- "Now, come on!" (said while laughing and gently pushing the guy's hand away)—The guy might think that she is flirting and playing games, not that she is setting a serious limit. The girl might worry that if she doesn't soften her response with a laugh or a playful spirit, she'll hurt the guy's feelings or turn him off completely.

- "Do you really think this is a good idea?"—Since the girl framed her statement as a question, the guy assumes that she is seeking his opinion, not that she is giving him a hidden message. Once again, the guy might feel that it's his job, as a "real man," to take responsibility for making all the sexual decisions for the two of them. By expressing her opinion in the form of a question, the woman is encouraging the man to think that she wants him to make the decision.

- "I'm not so sure about this."—Every good sales agent knows that many maybes can be turned into yeses if only he or she is persistent enough. By saying maybe when she really means no, the girl might be encouraging the guy to become more persistent when what she really wants is for him to back off.

Clear Communication

- "Please don't do that."—This is still a polite statement, but it leaves no room for misunderstanding. If the person who hears it doesn't give in to the request, it's always possible to repeat it. "I meant what I said—please don't do that."

- "I like kissing you a lot, but I don't want you to touch me there."—This statement says clearly what the person wants and what she doesn't want. It clearly tells the guy that the girl doesn't want to stop all sexual activity, just the particular activity that she has named.

- "I really like making out with you, but I don't want to go any further."—Again, the girl is saying clearly what she wants and what she doesn't want. She's specifying what she does want so that her positive statement can't be extended to cover something she didn't intend.

- Other ways of being clear:

  "I like your hand here, but not there."

  "I like you touching my breasts, but don't touch me down there."

  "*This* feels really good, but don't do *that*." (Make sure, though, that you are giving a clear physical demonstration of "this" and "that" so there's no confusion!)

- *Other ways of saying no:*

  "I don't want you to do that."

  "I don't like that."

  "That doesn't feel good."

  "I don't want to do that."

  "Stop that right now!"

  "If you keep going, this is rape."

Communication with Actions

Of course, we don't communicate through words alone. Sometimes we also communicate through actions.

A girl (or, in some cases, a guy) can communicate in this fashion by:

- refusing to go places where she might be alone with a guy;
- refusing to drink or take drugs;
- pushing a guy's hand away if he's touching her somewhere she doesn't want to be touched;
- hitting or kicking a guy who won't listen to more gentle messages.

Because of the communication problems we've been talking about, it's often a good idea to accompany some actions with serious words. Otherwise, a guy might think that a girl is just being playful, or worse, decide to match her physical actions with physical actions of his own. For example, if a girl pushes a guy's hand away, he might see that as token resistance—

something she is doing to prove that she's a "good girl," which she expects the guy to disregard. If she pushes his hand away while laughing and saying playfully, "Now, just stop it!" the guy might think she's just playing a game. In order to give a clear message, she might want to say what she wants in a serious fashion while acting on it.

Asking for More Information

It's not just up to girls to say no (or to boys, if they are the targets of sexual aggression). It's also up to boys (or aggressive girls) to ask for more information. That way, the more aggressive partner can be sure that he or she is really respecting the feelings of the other person, rather than assuming that everything will be all right if the more aggressive person just "plows ahead." Here are some ways of asking for more information:

- "Do you like it when I do this?"
- "Is this all right, or should I stop?"
- "Do you want me to go further?"
- "Tell me what you want," or "Tell me what you like."
- "Show me where you like to be touched."
- "Show me how you like to be touched."
- "I can't really tell what you want. Do you want me to keep doing this or not?"
- "If this isn't okay for you, I'll stop."

We believe communication should be a two-way street. It shouldn't really be up to only one partner to make sure that both people are communicating well. If a woman is uncomfortable with what her partner is doing, she should tell him in a clear and unmistakable way. That way, he never has to worry about going too far without realizing it.

However, in our society, as we've said, women often find it difficult to be that clear. So a man who wants to be sure that he's not causing a woman pain or discomfort might need to do some extra work in order to be sure of what she really wants. The payoff could be that both partners will feel more comfortable with each other sexually, so both people can enjoy more of what they actually do.

Getting Comfortable

In our society, men and women generally find it difficult to talk about sex with each other. This is frequently true even for adults who have been having sexual relationships for years. How much more true is it, then, for teenagers who are just starting out to explore sexuality and relationships.

Oddly enough, just knowing that it's hard to talk about sex and uncomfortable to communicate clearly about relationships can actually make it easier to talk. Either the guy or the girl might start a conversation by saying, "Look, I know this is hard to talk about, but I think we'll both feel better if we do it." Sometimes, talking about sex apart from the actual time of kissing or making out can help both partners feel secure about what's expected and what's acceptable. It can be hard to talk or to listen while you're feeling turned on—or worried about what your partner is going to do next!

On-the-Date Training

Sometimes the way a date goes can actually reinforce the message that a guy should ignore a girl's wishes. Both the guy and the girl can participate in this pattern. As we've said, if this pattern results in date rape, that's still the guy's responsibility. No matter what the girl has done, forcing her to have sex that she doesn't want is never justified. Nevertheless, it's to a girl's advantage to learn how to interrupt this pattern of "training" a guy to not listen to her. And for guys who genuinely respect girls and want to please them, it's helpful to understand how some girls give mixed or confusing messages.

Look at the following story of a date. What do you notice about the pattern that is being established?

Jamar picks Odessa up to take her to a party at the house of one of his friends. At the party, some of his friends all gather around her and start teasing her about the outfit she is wearing. They make remarks about her legs and her breasts, remarks that sound like compliments but that actually make Odessa very uncomfortable. But since these are Jamar's friends, she doesn't want to seem stuck-up or unfriendly, so she laughs and pretends to be flattered.

Later the guys get a little rowdier. They start spraying each other with beer cans, and some of the beer gets on Odessa. She really doesn't like this, but she still doesn't want to make a fuss. Once again, she pretends to be having a good time, even though in truth she's a little annoyed.

Jamar actually asks her if she's having a good time at the party, but Odessa doesn't want to tell him the truth. After all, she doesn't want to hurt his feelings, and she really wants him to like her. He seems to be having a good time, so she says she is, too.

Finally, Jamar says he is ready to leave, and he asks Odessa where she wants to go next. She says "Oh, anywhere you want." So Jamar drives them both to his house, where Odessa discovers that his family is out for the evening. Odessa would rather have gone out to a coffee shop or a restaurant, but when Jamar gets out a bottle of wine and two glasses, she helps him set up the wine on the coffee table by the couch. Jamar puts some music on the stereo and sits down next to Odessa on the couch. They have some wine and then they start kissing.

Odessa really likes kissing Jamar, but when he starts going further, sexually, she wants to stop. But she doesn't like to come right out and say, "Don't do that," so she asks him for some more wine. He gives her more wine, then starts making out with her again. Next Odessa tries to start a conversation about Jamar's plans for the summer, but Jamar just says, "We can talk later." Finally, Odessa has to come right out and say, "I really don't want to do this." Now Jamar is angry. He says,

"You've been coming on to me all evening! How can you expect me to stop now?"

Can you see how Odessa was actually "training" Jamar not to listen to her?

- When she didn't like Jamar's friends' sexual compliments, she smiled and acted like she did like them.
- When she didn't like Jamar's friends' treatment of her body—spraying her with beer—she smiled and went along.
- When Jamar asked her what she wanted to do, she said, "Anything you want," and when he took her to his empty house, she didn't object.
- When Jamar acted sexual with her in a way she wasn't comfortable with, she pretended that she wanted something else from him—more wine or conversation—rather than being clear about what she didn't like.

In other words, every time something happened that Odessa didn't like, she went along with it anyway. Every time Jamar asked her what she preferred, she told him to make the decisions. Jamar might have sensed her discomfort with the way his friends were treating her—but by going along with it, she gave him the message that it was all right not to take her seriously, to make sexual remarks to her, and to take liberties with her body. Jamar might have thought she had opinions and wishes of her own, but by saying "Anything you want," Odessa gave him the message that his feelings were much more important to her than her own.

Here's another scenario in which the girl is actually rewarding the guy for ignoring her wishes. Can you see how?

Luke drives Amy to a school dance. On the way, he takes some beer out of the trunk and offers her something to drink. Amy says, "I don't really like beer and I'm not sure you should be drinking while you're driving." Luke says, "Oh, don't be silly. I can handle it. Go on, have a beer. It will help you relax!" Amy has been wanting to go out with Luke for a long time, and it's really important to her to act like a good sport. She takes a couple of sips of beer, makes a face, and says, "Gee, that beer went right to my head! Guess I'd better not have any more." Luke laughs, but he doesn't make her drink any more beer, and Amy feels relieved.

At the dance, Luke holds Amy really close. At first she likes it, but then she gets embarrassed. She thinks sex should be private and she doesn't want her teachers to see her being this sexual with Luke. She doesn't want Luke to think she doesn't like him, though, so she says, "Hey, I need some fresh air. Can we go outside?" Luke takes her out to the parking lot and offers her another beer. Again Amy does her routine of drinking just a little, giggling, and pushing the beer away, and again Luke laughs at her. Amy is pleased that he seems to be having a good time.

When they go back on the dance floor, Luke is a little drunk, and he holds Amy closer than ever. Amy tries to pull away without him noticing, but that just makes him hold her in different ways that are even more sexual and even harder to get out of. Finally, Amy says, "You know, I'm kind of tired. Maybe we should go."

They get in the car, and Luke heads out toward the edge of town. Amy says, "Where are we going?" Luke says, "It's a surprise, just for you. I hope you like it!" Amy feels uncomfortable, but she loves the idea of a surprise "just for her," and she doesn't want to start an argument. She says "okay, but let's not stay out too late, okay? I really am kind of tired."

When Luke stops the car in an isolated place, Amy realizes that she is alone with him, that he's more drunk than she realized, and that she has no way of getting home except for him. When he starts kissing her and touching her in ways she doesn't like, she tries to push him away, but, just like on the dance floor, that just makes him hold her closer.

If the pattern that Luke and Amy have set up continues, Luke may very well end up forcing Amy to have sex. Every time Luke did something that Amy didn't like, she said no, but she said no in such a subtle way that Luke might not even have noticed her discomfort. Amy disguised her no about the beer by pretending to like drinking; she disguised her no about the sexual holding at the dance by asking to go outside; she disguised her no about going to an isolated place by saying okay, and then making up an excuse about not staying too late. In a way, she changed every one of her nos into yeses, giving Luke the message that if he just persisted long enough, he could get his own way about everything. In a sense, Amy was training Luke to ignore her wishes and her nos.

If women want to interrupt this pattern, they need to learn to communicate clearly, in some of the ways we talked about earlier in the chapter. If men want to interrupt it, they need to pay very careful attention to the women they're with and ask for clarification if they think the woman is giving a mixed or contradictory message. Both men and women can start training each other to be clear and to pay attention, rather than to set up a situation where one person is encouraged to ignore and overrule the other.

Giving Clear Messages to Acquaintances

Although acquaintance rape does not occur within the same circumstances as date rape, a lot of what we've been saying about good communication applies to both. The major difference is that when acquaintance rape takes place outside of a date, the man is much more likely to be aware that he is doing something out of bounds. A man who is going with a woman on a date may expect that she will willingly have sex with him, and he may rape her with the belief that she has already agreed to sex. A man who forces sex on a woman outside of a date is far less likely to believe that the woman has somehow agreed.

Nevertheless, women can be very clear with their acquaintances in the same way that we are suggesting they be very clear with their dates. Say, for example, that Ellen had been able to speak up clearly about what was making her uncomfortable. Suppose she had been able to tell the meter man that she didn't want him to sit so close to her, or suppose she had clearly asked him to leave when she started feeling funny about his being there. Although there's no guarantee that this behavior would have protected her, clear communication might have made a difference. At the very least, it would have meant Ellen was standing up for herself and what she wanted—behavior that might have helped her later on, even if the situation did get worse.

Women may feel reluctant to protect themselves from acquaintance rape for the same reasons that they find it hard to protect themselves from date rape. In both cases, they may be doing what they have been trained to do—putting a man's feelings ahead of their own, being more concerned with making another person feel comfortable than with doing what makes them feel comfortable. The fears of being rude, of hurting someone's feelings, or of provoking a man's anger, may keep a woman from clear communication with male acquaintances as well as with dates.

Part of the risk of communicating clearly is that the other person may really not want to hear what you want to say. Women are often trained to believe that if they just say something in the right way, the other person won't notice that there's a disagreement, just as men are often trained to believe that if there *is* a disagreement, the person who is most persistent deserves to win. In order to interrupt the patterns that produce acquaintance rape, women may have to be willing to make other people uncomfortable and to live with the anger, irritation, resentment, or rejection that sometimes results. The good news is that once you are willing to stand up for yourself, you may discover that other people's reactions don't bother you nearly as much as you thought they would.

Who Is a Rapist?

In the early 1970s, Susan Brownmiller wrote a groundbreaking book about rape called *Against Our Will*. In it, she made the point that rape is not really a crime about sex. Rather, it is a crime of power. Ultimately, she argued, a man rapes a woman not so much because he wants to have sex with her as because he wants to prove that he is more powerful than she is.

In his book *Men Who Rape*, Nicholas Groth describes three types of rapists who fit Brownmiller's analysis: the power rapist, the anger rapist, and the sadist. The *power rapist* is most purely interested in exercising his own power. He will generally use only just as much force as needed to make sure a woman does what he wants. If the woman doesn't struggle, he won't hurt her. If she does struggle, he'll hurt her as much as necessary to get his own way.

The *anger rapist* is generally acting out strong feelings of anger against women, usually going back to a troubled relationship with his mother. He may see rape as an act of revenge on women who have laughed at him, humiliated him, battered him, or hurt him in some other way. He may see rape as a justified punishment for a woman. Or his anger may be so overwhelming that he feels out of control, like a child having a tantrum—except, of course, that he has much more physical strength than a child does, and a far greater power to do harm.

The *sadist rapist* is particularly interested in making women (or sometimes men) suffer. Frequently this type of rapist will kill or mutilate his targets after he has committed sexual acts. He may also be specifically interested in humiliating his targets or making them suffer in some other way.

Any of these types of rapists might rape a woman while on a date. They might also rape acquaintances or strangers, or they might rape women in many different situations, depending on the rapist's personality and situation.

A "gray area" in date rape involves men who find women's helplessness sexy. Such men might be turned on by a woman who was too drunk or stoned to say no or to resist effectively.

However, in addition to men who fit the profile of "rapists," there are many "non-rapist" men who nevertheless commit date rape. These are the men who genuinely don't notice they are forcing a woman into a sexual act against her will. Or they believe that the woman wants to be forced (like Scarlett O'Hara), or that they are justified by her behavior in forcing her. Because these "non-rapist" men aren't driven by their personalities to assert their power by raping, they can learn to stop committing date rape if they learn how to understand the problem differently.

Why do otherwise "non-rapist" men find themselves committing date rape? Researchers like Andrea Parrot believe that these men don't start out a date intending to rape. Rather, they go out on a date expecting to have sex. If the woman they're with wants to have sex, they have no need to rape (unlike the "rapist" men, who actually *want* to force a woman against her will, in order to feel their power). But if their date doesn't want to have sex, they may feel justified forcing her.

We believe that in many cases of date rape, both sex and power are involved. The man often starts out the evening expecting that he will have sex, that he has a "right" to sex, and his expectation is so strong that he may commit rape without even realizing that he has done so. Certainly power is involved in this act, but so is simple misunderstanding. If these "non-rapist" men can learn to see dates differently, they can control their behavior fairly easily. Men who fit the profile of "rapist," on the other hand, are driven by all sorts of psychological needs to assert their power over women in cruel and painful ways. Treatment for this condition is rigorous and highly specialized, and its success is very limited and not at all guaranteed or even likely.

Defending Yourself

Sad to say, there are no foolproof ways for a woman to protect herself against date rape. That's because, as we have seen, the patterns that lead to date rape are on a continuum with "normal" dating behavior and because men who are not really rapists may wind up committing date rape under certain circumstances. Likewise, there are no foolproof ways for a woman to protect herself against acquaintance rape. That's because, once again, the type of behavior that may lead to acquaintance rape is on a continuum with accepted male-female behavior.

However, even if there are no formulas, there are several danger signs to watch out for. There are also various suggestions that experts have made for dealing with various types of men who rape.

Danger Signs of Date Rape

The following are elements in a date to watch out for, especially if a girl doesn't know her date very well:

Isolation. If a woman is all alone with a man, whether in his house, her house, his car, or in some isolated spot, she has far fewer resources to protect herself if the man goes further than she'd like, sexually. Isolation also includes situations where the woman is surrounded by the man's friends, who might support him rather than her in a conflict over sex.

Dependence. A woman who needs a man to drive her home will have a lot harder time standing up for herself than a woman with money to take a taxi, access to another ride home, or the ability to take public transportation or to walk. If a woman sets things up so that she can take

more difficult for her to demand that her date respect her feelings and preferences.

In chapter 2, we talked about some other factors contributing to women's low self-esteem. Generally, to the extent that a woman feels good about herself, she'll find it easier to stand up for what she wants, right from the beginning of the evening. If she's in a position where she wants to say no to a man's sexual behavior, her positive feelings about herself will put more force behind her nos, helping her to give clearer messages. If you feel you have difficulties valuing yourself as much as you deserve, you might want to find some ways to improve your self-image. Possibly you might want to talk to a counselor or some other professional "helper," such as a minister, priest, or rabbi.

"Ladylike" Behavior

As we've seen in several chapters, traditional ideas about "ladylike" behavior don't go well with protecting oneself from date rape. A traditional "lady" never raises her voice, puts her own wishes first, or makes other people feel uncomfortable. A woman who wants to protect herself from date or acquaintance rape may need to do some or all of these things.

Furthermore, a woman who believes she should be a "lady" may feel guilty or anxious about her own sexual feelings, which traditionally a "lady" isn't supposed to have. These uncomfortable feelings may make it harder for a woman to stand up for herself and harder to believe that she has the right to do whatever she wants sexually—as well as the right to say no to whatever she wants.

If you feel that your ideas of ladylike behavior are getting in the way or protecting yourself, you might want to read, think, and talk more about your ideas of being a "lady" and being a "woman." Maybe there's a women's studies class at your school you could take, or perhaps you could find a teacher who is interested in helping you and your friends start a discussion group. Maybe you could find support or information at a local community center, YWCA or YWHA, or women's group in the area.

Survivors of Sexual Abuse

Some girls reach their teenage years with a history of being sexually abused—of having sexual relationships forced on them by men (or sometimes women) in or close to their families. Sometimes, too, these sexually abusive relationships continue throughout the teenage years.

Girls with this type of history have in effect been raped before, sometimes several times, often by people they loved or were close to. Sad to say, this may make it easier for them to be raped again, particularly by people they care about or feel close to, because girls with this history have been taught that they cannot, or don't deserve to, protect themselves from unwanted sexual contact. Not being able to keep fathers, stepfathers, or other male or female relatives from abusing them may have given them the message that they are not able to keep any man from abusing them. This may make it difficult for them to read the signals warning them that their date or acquaintance is a potential rapist or to act on their own behalf even if they do read the signals.

If a girl has a history of being sexually abused, or if she's still being raped or abused by people she's close to, we urge her to get counseling or some other kind of help to support her in dealing with the problem and ending the abuse. Meanwhile, we encourage her to get whatever support she needs in dealing with the people she dates, to help her insist on healthy, loving relationships in every aspect of her life.

How Boys Can Defend Themselves Against Sexual Aggression

Most of the suggestions that we have made for girls throughout this chapter apply to boys as well. Boys can also learn how to say clearly what they want and don't want, to develop the self-esteem they need to assert and protect themselves, to recognize situations in which women—or other men—repeatedly show that they do not respect their wishes or their feelings.

Boys can also help prevent sexual aggression by thinking through their own ideas about sex, relationships, and manliness. If a guy buys into the concept that "real men" are ready for sex all the time, that men are always stronger than women, or that men have a duty to satisfy women, he will find it much harder to defend himself against sexual aggression. If a guy is interested in being with other men sexually, but feels guilty or uncomfortable about those feelings, he will also have a harder time making decisions that feel good to him. If, on the other hand, a guy has figured out what *he* wants from women, other men, sex, and relationships, and is comfortable with his own feelings, he'll have a much easier time standing up for himself.

Sexual Decision Making

If we were to end this chapter leaving you with only one message, it would be to encourage you to think through your own ideas about what kind of person you want to be and what kind of relationships you want to have—and then to take action to make your ideas come true.

This is not an easy task. Sex roles in our society are very specifically defined. Although in some ways there is a lot of confusion, in other ways sex roles are very rigid. Learning to make decisions about your sexuality and your relationships can feel lonely, frightening, or upsetting—as well as exciting, liberating, and comforting. It may be tempting to make decisions by default: to "just say no" because you're a "good girl"; to try to "score" because you're a "real man." Members of both sexes might be tempted to get drunk or high as a way of avoiding clear decision making. Not communicating with your partner is another way of evading decisions, because by not telling your partner what you want, you are letting him or her make the decisions for you.

Pressures on both sexes can be very painful, especially during the teenage years, as young people try to figure out their identities—their personal likes, dislikes, values, and principles. The search for your own identity is one of the biggest challenges of this time of your life—but if you've got the courage and the determination to stick with it, it can be one of the most rewarding processes you'll ever know.

6

Coping with Date and Acquaintance Rape

Just because a rape takes place on a date or with an acquaintance rather than on a street with a stranger doesn't make it any less of a violent crime. The physical and emotional trauma of rape is the same whether a woman was raped by a stranger, an acquaintance, or a man she was romantically involved with. In fact, date rape is particularly traumatic in that it calls into question the woman's judgment and the woman's social circles in a new and particularly disturbing way. Acquaintance rape may likewise make a woman feel that she can't trust *any* man, or that she can't trust her own judgment.

In this chapter, we'll talk about some of the aftereffects of date and acquaintance rape and about some of the kinds of help that women may need, as well as about ways in which men can cope with date rape and sexual aggressors. We'll also talk about ways in which all people can take action to help stop date rape. For more specific suggestions on where to learn more or to find help, see chapter 7.

Medical Attention

A woman who has been raped should seek medical attention as soon as possible. To some extent, this is for her own immediate protection. She needs to make sure there is no physical damage that she's not aware of, such as tears in the lining of her vagina or other types of internal damage. She may also need to get tested for pregnancy and for sexually transmitted diseases, particularly if the rapist did not use a condom. The prospect that there may be medical aftereffects of an already traumatic experience adds further emotional pain to an already upsetting experience.

Although pregnancy is not a common result of rape, it does occur. A woman might want to take a morning-after pill, which will act to terminate any pregnancy that may have started. This treatment can be given within 72 hours after the rape, before the results of a pregnancy test are in. Its side effects include nausea and other after-effects of taking a pill with high doses of female hormones. A woman interested in this treatment should discuss the side effects with her doctor. An actual pregnancy test won't show results until some weeks later; a woman may wait to make decisions about pregnancy until that time.

Sexually transmitted diseases will not show any symptoms for some weeks at least. A person infected with HIV, the virus that causes AIDS, may not have any symptoms for several years. A woman who has gotten gonorrhea or syphilis may have no symptoms or only slight ones within a few weeks followed by no symptoms at all for months or years. However, these diseases can be tested for fairly soon after the event through simple blood tests. There is no time limit on when these tests can be taken, but the sooner they are taken the better, in order to treat any diseases that have been acquired and in order to protect future partners against these diseases. The exception to this is AIDS, where antibodies can take at least six months, and often longer to appear on tests. With AIDS, one encounter with an HIV-positive person may or may not infect the partner; many factors are involved. Anyone who is raped should consider being tested at the appropriate time to be certain.

The myths about sexually transmitted diseases say that only lowlifes or poor people get them. In fact, anyone can have one of these diseases, particularly if he or she has had sex with a lot of people. A date rapist is likely to have had a large number of sexual partners, as is a woman who commits sexual aggression against a man; therefore, these people are likely to be at a higher risk of sexually transmitted diseases, even if they are rich, seem healthy, and are well educated.

Legal Evidence

Another reason to seek medical attention is for evidence in case the woman ever wants to take legal action against her rapist. The medical evidence collected right after the rape can be used in a trial or other legal proceeding.

Many women's first reaction after a rape is to want to take care of themselves, not to turn to others for help. After all, they've just had an experience that makes it very difficult to trust others, particularly the men who are most likely to predominate in a medical setting. A woman might want to take a shower, change her torn or dirty clothes, douche, or in other ways act to remove the evidence of her rape.

It is very important not to act on these impulses if a woman has any intention of seeking legal recourse for what happened. Police and medical personnel need to see the woman in exactly the state in which the rapist left her so that this evidence can be used at a trial. A woman who wants to preserve evidence should not wash, douche, gargle, brush her teeth, comb her hair, or change her clothes.

However, the first priority for every rape survivor must be to take care of herself. Sometimes it's still possible to go to trial without physical evidence after a date rape, because the date rapist may admit that sexual intercourse took place. then the legal issue becomes whether or not the woman consented.

Emotional Effects of Getting Medical Help

Sad to say, because of the myths about rape, acquaintance rape, and date rape in our society, medical personnel are not always sensitive and caring in their treatment of rape survivors. Consciously or unconsciously, they may not take the trauma of rape seriously, or they may give the woman the message that it was "her fault." Or they may simply be busy and preoccupied, so that the woman who felt helpless at the hands of her rapist now feels pushed around, ignored, or turned into an "object" by the doctor, nurse, physician's assistant, or medical social worker who is supposed to be helping her.

If possible, a woman who has been raped should get a friend or advocate to go with her while she gets medical attention. That way, there is at least one person in the situation whom she trusts and to whom she can turn for help and care. Many towns and cities have rape crisis centers that can be called 24 hours a day. These centers offer telephone counseling at the very least; frequently they will send someone to accompany a rape survivor through the medical and legal processes that follow a rape. These services are usually anonymous, which means that the rape survivor does not have to give the center her name. Rape crisis counselors are experienced in dealing with people after rape; frequently they have survived rape themselves, so they know from personal experience what a woman is going through. They also have experience dealing assertively with doctors, other medical personnel, and police.

Emotional Effects of Rape

Immediately after a rape, most survivors suffer from something called *rape trauma syndrome*. This is a series of three phases through which the person tries to take in what happened, to accept it, and to readjust.

The first phase is called the *acute* or *crisis* phase, which can last for days or even longer. In this phase, the person who has been raped struggles with the fact that she was powerless to protect herself from an upsetting attack. Since this is a painful fact to accept, people cope with it in different ways. Some people are immediately in touch with their feelings of anger at the rapist. Other people feel guilty, turning their anger on themselves. ("I should have known better! How could I have been so stupid? there must be something wrong with me!")

Some people in this phase seem unnaturally calm or carefree, as though nothing had happened at all. They may be trying to turn off all their feelings so they won't feel how upset they are about the rape. Or they may be trying to replace their painful feelings with pleasant ones. People who deal with rape in this way may not fit other people's idea of how a person should behave after this crime. It's important to see this calm or carefree behavior as a woman's way of dealing with a terrible experience, not as a sign that the experience wasn't so bad or even that the woman welcomed the rape.

Generally, rape survivors report feeling powerlessness, shock, guilt, depression, anxiety, shame, embarrassment, and disbelief during this phase. However, they may have great difficulty getting in touch with these feelings or expressing them to others.

After the body and the emotions have coped with the initial shock of being raped, the survivor may enter the second phase, *disorientation.* This is where defenses start to break down, now that the emergency is over. During this period, a survivor may not be sure how to act. She may have trouble connecting to other people or even having a casual conversation. She may try to forget that the rape ever happened. She might give up dating, so that she can "never be raped again," or she may be afraid to leave home, since "outside" was where she was raped. A person may be afraid of triggering the memory of the rape, so she may limit her contact with other people or her activities in general.

Finally, the survivor starts to put herself back together again during the *reorientation* phase. Now she feels stronger and can begin to deal with the memory of the rape. Rape survivors report that the experience of a rape never completely leaves them, but that there are ways of going on to a happy and loving future. A woman may go on to feel different about strangers, about the men she dates, about certain types of men, or men in general. She may handle herself differently on dates, in public, or even in private with people she does or doesn't know well. However, she may also learn new ways of taking care of herself, and she may feel strong in the knowledge that she has been through a very difficult experience and survived.

If a woman does not get counseling and/or good support from relatives and friends, she may never reach the reorientation phase. She may be so upset by the painful memory of the rape that she continues to try to forget it rather than make it a part of her life and go on. Getting counseling and good support from the people in her life is extremely important to a rape survivor.

Getting Help

Often one of the most difficult parts of a rape comes afterward, when a woman tries to put her life back together again. During that time, it can help to talk to friends and family—but these people can sometimes be unhelpful or even make things worse.

Sometimes people are so upset by the idea of a rape that they become overwhelmed by their own feelings. A woman who has been raped deserves to have her own feelings be the focus of any discussion of the event, rather than the feelings of the person she's talking to. A friend or family member may feel overwhelmed with anger, guilt, frustration, pain, anxiety, embarrassment, or shame. He or she may blame himself/herself, or the person might deal with upsetting feelings by putting the blame on the rape survivor ("You should have known better! You should have done something different!").

If you are a rape survivor who is having this experience with a friend or family member, remember: *You don't have to talk with anyone who doesn't make you feel better*. Even if you did not have the power to say no to your rapist, you do have the power to say no to the people in your life who are not being helpful to you. You don't have to worry about their feelings or their needs. You have a right to focus on your own.

Worries

Many rape survivors worry that a rape means something bad about them, either something so bad that everyone can see it or a hidden bad thing that someone could find out after getting to know them better. Although a rape means only that a person has had a bad experience, it's hard not to take that bad experience and turn it into something bigger. Here are some of the things that rape survivors often worry about:

- Now I'm no longer a virgin
- I don't have the right to refuse sex with anyone else
- I don't have the power to refuse sex with anyone else
- I'll never enjoy sex again
- Everyone can see what I am
- It was all my fault—I should never have (let him in the door, dressed that way, been nice to him, gotten drunk, gone out with him, let him give me a ride home, let him see how excited I was, etc., etc., etc.)
- I'll never be able to trust a man again

Of course, being raped doesn't logically lead to any of the "facts" on that list. A person who has been raped may not have the medical evidence of her virginity—the hymen or maidenhead in front of the vagina—but lot's of women who haven't had sex don't have this evidence either. The idea of being a virgin has more to do with a person's choices than with what has been done to her.

Certainly a person who has been forced to have sex has the right to say no to another sexual encounter, just as a person who has agreed to sex has the right to say no another time. And just because a person was raped does not mean she has lost all her power or that she can't protect herself in other situations.

Many rape survivors do report emotional difficulties with sex and with trusting men, but this is not everybody's experience. Even if it is your experience, it does not have to last the rest of your life. If these issues concern you, counseling can go a long way toward helping you overcome fear and other problems that get in the way of forming good sexual relationships.

No one can tell by looking at a person if he or she is the victim of a violent crime, whether the crime is rape, theft, or some other form of attack. What may be visible is the person's sense of fear, shame, or anger—although no one will know the reason for it. The sooner a rape survivor allows herself to feel all of the painful feelings that surround a rape, the sooner those feelings will pass and she can get on with her life. Once again, counseling can be extremely helpful in moving through these difficult feelings.

Blaming oneself is a very common aftereffect of rape, especially date or acquaintance rape. It's very painful to believe that we absolutely could not control something bad that was happening to us. Sometimes it's less painful to believe that we, not the uncontrollable force, were at fault. However, in the end, it's better to be accurate about what happened. The rapist is at fault for the rape. Even if the rape survivor showed extremely bad judgment, she did not commit a crime—he did.

Possibly a rape survivor did show bad judgment and will want to change her behavior in the future. Possibly she showed no bad judgment but wants to decide that she did, so that she has the illusion of control later on. For example, she may decide that she should never take another drink again, since liquor was involved in her rape. Rationally speaking, there may be good reasons to be careful about drinking, but avoiding liquor does not guarantee a person won't be raped. Making a magical "protection" can actually help keep a person from improving her judgment, since she has the feeling that she's already solved the problem.

Likewise, deciding not to date or not to trust any man may seem like a rational solution to the feelings of powerlessness and anger that can follow a date rape. And in fact, a rape survivor might want to examine her own judgment. Or she may conclude that her judgment was really not at fault. Either way, she needs to find a way to continue to date and to relate to others sexually, rather than shutting down in order to protect herself.

Finding people who can help her sort out truth from fantasy, good judgment from bad judgment, real solutions from false ones, is a high priority for rape survivors. Counselors, teachers, and sympathetic adults may be helpful here. Because they are close to a rape survivor, friends and family may be more wrapped up in their own feelings of pain or in their own need to protect the rape survivor—or they may be just the help and support that the person needs. Every rape survivor will have to make her own decisions about getting the help she deserves.

A Word About Counseling

There are two types of counseling the rape survivor may want to look into: short-term and long-term. Short-term counseling lasts from a few days to a few months. It is specifically designed to cope with the effects of a rape and the recovery process afterward. The rape survivor will talk about her feelings with a sympathetic counselor, who may offer specific suggestions for recovery.

Long-term counseling lasts from a few months to several years. It generally focuses on the underlying issues in a person's life, issues that a traumatic event like a rape may bring up. For example, if a woman has generally felt powerless in her life, being raped may bring these feelings to the surface in a dramatic way. As the effects of the rape itself fade, the woman may need help in coping with the feelings she had even before the rape, feelings that are even stronger now. Addressing these feelings may require going back and talking about how and where they started, as well as learning new perspectives on how to see one's life.

A long-term counselor usually does a lot more listening than talking. He or she may make some suggestions for the person's life, but usually this type of counselor is more concerned with helping the person get in touch with her own feelings and finding her own solutions. You can contact your local social services agency, rape crisis center, hospital, doctor, minister, priest, rabbi, or school counselor for suggestions on how to get counseling. Counseling can be expensive, especially long-term, but there are generally ways to find free or low-cost services.

Rape crisis centers or other agencies may also offer support groups for rape survivors. In support groups, a survivor gets the chance to meet other people who have been through what she has been through, and to hear how they are handling their lives now that the crisis is over. Many rape survivors find support groups to be extremely helpful in overcoming their sense of mistrust and isolation. A person can go to a support group for a sense of community as well as to a counselor for individual attention.

Legal Remedies

Generally, the legal system is not very kind to targets of rape, and it is the most difficult for survivors of date rape. Because of the myths we've discussed throughout this book, many people tend to blame women for being attacked, in ways that they would never dream of blaming a person whose car was stolen or whose house was broken into. Suppose a person left his car running on a busy downtown street, with the keys in the ignition and the doors unlocked. Clearly, this person would have shown extremely bad judgment, yet no jury in the world would refuse to convict the person who stole that man's car or give the thief a lighter sentence on the grounds that the car owner was "asking for it" or "behaving provocatively."

A person who brings charges against her date or acquaintance rapist may have to answer questions about her personal sexual life as well as giving a detailed story about what happened to her before, during, and after the rape. She may be accused of "asking for it" or mocked and insulted in other ways by the rapist's lawyer, whose job is to get his or her client off without punishment. Because a person does not have to testify against himself or herself in our legal system, the rapist may not even speak out in court, while the rape survivor will be put on the witness stand.

Because a rapist has broken the law, he theoretically should be tried in a *criminal court*—a place for people who break the law—but frequently this does not take place. Many rape cases never come to trial, either because the police are unsympathetic and don't report the rape to the district attorney (the lawyer charged with prosecuting people who commit crimes) or because the district attorney doesn't believe that the case can be won.

A person who has been raped can also take her case to *civil court*, in which disputes between people are resolved. If the rape survivor sues her rapist for causing her pain and distress, she may be able to take the case to civil court. In this case, she will have to hire her own lawyer to represent her.

Generally, experts in rape and counseling have mixed feelings about legal remedies. On the one hand, rape survivors often don't get treated well by the police, the courts, and the legal system in general. The traumatic experiences in this arena can extend and deepen the trauma of the original rape.

On the other hand, until rapists start being prosecuted and found guilty, many men will not take seriously a woman's power to say no and to defend herself. A rapist who is not prosecuted has full license to go out and attack some other woman. And some women experience a sense of empowerment in fighting back through the legal system, showing that even if they could not prevent the rape, at least they can respond to it.

Whether or not to seek legal remedies for rape is a very personal decision for every rape survivor. If you are considering seeking legal remedies, make sure you find someone to explain to you fully what is likely to happen and how strong your case is. A rape counselor, sympathetic lawyer, or police official may be able to help you understand what you can expect from taking legal action.

Counseling for Rapists and Sexual Aggressors

If you are someone who has committed rape or sexual aggression, you might also have a wide range of feelings about what you've done. You may have realized afterward that you forced another person into a painful or damaging situation; you may have even realized that you have a pattern of hurting other people in this way. You may have genuinely believed that you weren't doing anything wrong, only to discover that you actually did do harm to another person. Or you might have been aware that you were doing harm but have different feelings about acting that way.

Whatever your experiences, you should know that help and counseling are available to you, too. In fact, getting the help and support you deserve is the best way to ensure that in the future, your actions won't cause the same kind of harm. Guilt, shame, embarrassment, and anger can be powerful barriers to getting help—but if you can get past these defensive feelings, you might find that you actually feel better talking about your experiences, and you might start to see new ways of behaving opening up to you. Support groups as well as individual counseling are available to men who rape. Check with your local social agency, rape crisis center, or school counselor.

When Boys Are the Target

A boy who has been the target of date rape or sexual aggression is in a very difficult position. Because of the prejudices in our legal system, it will be very difficult for him to take any legal action. It may be difficult for him to find friends or family to support his feelings, since may people may deny that men can ever be forced into uncomfortable or damaging sexual situations.

Furthermore, the boy himself may not realize that anything bad has happened to him, even though he experiences feelings of guilt, mistrust, self-blame, shame, anger, and other typical feelings of rape survivors. Because there is almost no name for what has happened to him, he may feel isolated, even from himself, in dealing with it.

Fortunately, more counselors are becoming familiar with the issues of date rape and sexual aggression, as they affect both men and women. A boy who has been the target of sexual aggression or rape may have a harder time finding help, but if he persists, he can succeed.

Taking Action

As we have seen, rape doesn't exist in a vacuum. It exists in a climate where women aren't valued as much as men, where people of both sexes treat each other as objects, where "might makes right" and the tendency to blame the victim is a powerful one.

Looking at this climate and at the widespread problem of rape may feel overwhelming at times. But in fact there is a lot that each of us can do, alone and with others, to help prevent date and acquaintance rape and to change the climate in which it occurs. Following are some suggestions. Can you think of others?

- Get your school to sponsor an assembly, workshop, or class on date and acquaintance rape. Invite guest speakers from the local rape crisis center or social service agency. Put up posters and distribute books, pamphlets, or articles about the problem.
- Volunteer at a local rape crisis center—or get together with a community group and start one.
- When you hear a joke that turns women or men into objects, say something about it. Don't let it pass.
- Examine your own ideas about dating, relationships, men, and women. Read a new book on the subject, get into a discussion with friends, start a study or discussion group, or talk about it with your boyfriend or girlfriend. Decide whether you're happy with your personal rules about who should ask for a date, who should pay, and who should make decisions. Figure out how to make your actual practice fit more with what you believe.
- Get your school to sponsor an assembly, discussion group, or class on the bigger issues of women's equality or men's and women's roles. Once people start talking about a problem, they often come up with new solutions.

Date and acquaintance rape are painful and difficult subjects that affect many women and men in traumatic and upsetting ways. The good news, though, is that by becoming aware of these types of rape, we can change both the specific facts of this crime and the climate that helps the crime to occur. Whether or not you have been personally involved in date or acquaintance rape, you can make a difference in helping to end it and in preventing it in the future.

7

Where to Find Help

The following organizations provide help or information in dealing with issues of date rape—especially its prevention and treatment.

Anti Social and Violent Behavior Center
301-443-3728
Has directory of rape crisis centers and hot lines in the Washington, D.C. area

Battered Women's Alternatives
P.O. Box 6406
Concord, CA 94524
510-676-2845 (office)
888-215-5555 (24-hour hot line)

Community Counseling Centers of Chicago
4740 North Clark Street
Chicago, IL 60640
773-769-0205

Domestic Abuse Project (DAP)
204 West Franklin
Minneapolis, MN 55404
612-874-7063
612-646-0994 (women's 24-hour hot line)
612-379-6363 (men's 24-hour hot line)

Men Stopping Rape
306 North Brooks Street
Madison, WI 53715
608-257-4444
Community-based group of men seeking ways to end masculine violence. Educates about male socialization, destructive masculinity, homophobia, and racism

National Coalition Against Sexual Assault (NCASA)
125 North Enola Drive
Enola, PA 17025
717-728-9764

National Coalition Against Sexual Assault (NCASA)
Ending Violence Effectively
P.O. Box 18212
Denver, CO 80218
303-322-7010

National Domestic Violence Hotline
800-799-7233
800-787-3224 (TTY)

Portland Women's Crisis Line
P.O. Box 42610
Portland, OR 97242
503-235-5333

Rape Assistance and Awareness Program
P.O. Box 18951

Denver, CO 80218
303-329-9922

Rape Crisis Center of Central Massachusetts
146 West Boylston Street
Worcester, MA 01606
508-852-7600 (office)
508-799-5700 (24-hour hot line)
800-870-5905
800-223-5001 (24-hour Spanish hot line)

Sexual Assault Care Center
76 Grenville
Toronto, Canada M5S 1B2
416-323-6040
416-323-6300 (24-hour hot line)

Other resources include a local rape crisis center (found under "Rape" or "Rape Crisis" in a phone book or directory assistance); the local YWCA; a local suicide prevention hot line; the local police (who may have a rape crisis unit); or your school's counseling center.

For Further Reading

Bateman, Py. *Acquaintance Rape: Awareness and Prevention for Teenagers*. Seattle: Alternatives to Fear, 1982, 24 pages. A book emphasizing prevention of acquaintance rape, focusing on signals that might indicate possible danger.

————. *Macho: Is That What You Really Want?* Seattle: Alternatives to Fear, 1986. A book for boys only, to help them find new ways to deal with girls and new ways to cope with pressure from their male friends. Both Bateman titles are available from: Alternatives to Fear, 2811 East Madison, Suite #208, Seattle, WA 98112

Benedict, Helen. *Recovery: How to Survive Sexual Assault for Women, Men, Teenagers, and Their Friends and Families*. New York: Doubleday, 1988. Takes you through every step of the process of recovery from rape and other sexual assaults, with a focus on practical information.

————. *Safe, Strong and Streetwise: The Teenager's Guide to Sexual Assault*. Boston: Joy Street Books, 1986. Gives suggestions for safety in situations that might lead to rape

Parrot, Andrea. *Coping With Date Rape & Acquaintance Rape*. New York: The Rosen Publishing Group, 1988. A wide-ranging look at date rape and acquaintance rape.

Warshaw, Robin. *I Never Called It Rape*. New York: Harper-Collins Publishers, 1988. A book based on first-person accounts taken from studies conducted on college campuses by a freelance journalist, Warshaw, who draws a portrait of men who rape women whom they know.

INDEX